THE OTTOMAN EMPIRE
a brief history

'In Brief' Series: Books for Busy People

by Anne Davison

Cover design by Karen Turner

Other books by the same author

A History of China

A History of Russia

Abraham's Children: Jew, Christian Muslim, Commonality and Conflict

From the Medes to the Mullahs: a History of Iran

Making Sense of Militant Islam

Paul of Tarsus: a First Century Radical

The Holy Roman Empire: Power Politics Papacy

The Mughal Empire

http://www.inbriefbooks.com

TABLE OF CONTENTS

MAPS

PROLOGUE

Many books have been written about the Ottoman Empire. Some of these are scholarly works written by academics. Others focus on one particular period of Ottoman history or perhaps a particular geographic area.

This book is different in that it is written for the general reader, covers the entire period of some six hundred years, and assumes no prior knowledge.

The history of the Ottoman Empire, as with most Empires, is complex. It is also a history that is little understood by the general public. At the same time there are many events that occurred within the context of Ottoman history that the general reader may be quite familiar with: for example, the Fall of Constantinople in 1453, the Crimean War in 1853, the Battle of Gallipoli or exploits of Lawrence of Arabia during the First World War.

Although all Ottoman history is fascinating, the period from the 18th Century onwards is particularly important in relation to the making of today's Eastern Europe and the Balkans. Equally, if not more importantly, is the period from the First World War and the dissolution of the Empire. A better understanding of this last period could help many people make more sense of the complex situation in the Middle East today.

The aim of this book is to offer a general overview of what is a complex history of the many countries and cultures that made up the Ottoman Empire while at the same time placing some of the more familiar events within their historical context. It is rather like putting small pieces of a jigsaw into their correct place while not losing sight of the big picture.

While there will inevitably be gaps in a work of this size it is hoped that the reader may be inspired to further reading on the subject. For those interested a short selection of the main works that have been consulted is provided at the end of the text.

As with other books in the 'In Brief' series, this book is aimed at the general reader who wants to understand a particular historical topic but does not have the time or inclination to read a heavy academic tome. With this in mind, footnotes have been omitted.

Finally, I would like to thank those friends and colleagues who gave of their time to read through various chapters, proof read the script, and offered helpful comments.

INTRODUCTION

The Ottoman Empire was officially founded in 1299 when Osman I became the first Sultan. It was abolished in November 1922 in the aftermath of the First World War. At its peak, during the reign of Suleiman the Magnificent in the 16th Century, the Empire covered an area that included North Africa and Arabia, the Balkans, today's Turkey, Syria and the Levant. During the same period the Ottoman army was both feared and respected by Western powers and the Ottoman navy competed on an equal footing with the Genoese and Venetians for mastery of the Mediterranean Sea. In 1529, when Suleiman led his armies right up to the walls of Vienna, panic seized the hearts of Christians in Europe and as the Turkish armies gradually moved westwards many feared that an Islamic conquest would lead to the demise of Christendom in Western Europe.

The founder of the Empire, Osman I, belonged to the Oghuz tribe. The Oghuzs were a Turkic speaking people who migrated from the region of Kazakhstan in Central Asia to Anatolia during the 13th Century. Having brought the various Seljuk tribes of Anatolia under their influence, the Ottomans then went on to conquer much of the Balkans, the Levant, parts of Arabia and the coastal regions of North Africa. In this way the Empire became multi-national, multi-lingual and multi-religious.

The Ottomans were Sunni Muslims and for much of the Empire's history, although non-Muslims were subject to certain discriminatory legislation, there was never a policy aimed at their conversion to Islam. Religious communities were generally permitted to practice their faith and organise their own internal affairs in return for the payment of a special government tax (*jyziah* tax).

By the 18th Century the Ottomans were falling well behind Europe in terms of trade and industry. Valuable trade was lost due to new markets opening up in the Far East supported by the British and

Dutch East India Companies. Home markets suff
generous trade concessions being granted by th
European countries. At the same time the Empire
modernisation and industrialisation met fierce resistance ɪɪ ʋɪɪ.
conservative clerics. Western observers often blamed this
situation on the traditional conservatism of Islam. The lack of
modernisation and the cost of the Balkan wars led the Empire into
debt and it was in this context that the Ottoman Empire became
known in the West as the 'Sick Man of Europe'.

During the 19th Century parts of the Empire, with encouragement
from the Western powers, began to seek self-rule. This was
particularly the case in the Balkans, an area that was largely
populated by Christians. Russia, for example, sought special
concessions from the Ottomans on the grounds that she had a
duty to protect her co-religionists, the Orthodox Christians and
particularly those living in Greece, Serbia and the Holy Land.
Austria also claimed a special relationship with the populations of
countries such as Hungary and Croatia based on the principle they
were all Roman Catholic. Both Russia and Austria would later
argue that they had a right to intervene in Ottoman affairs in
defence of persecuted Christians.

Throughout the 19th and early 20th Centuries nationalistic fervour
and calls for independence spread across Eastern Europe and the
Balkans. These anti-Ottoman uprisings were often supported by
Austria and Russia as each competed for territorial influence in
the region. Britain and France, who were wary of Russian
expansionism, also became involved in Ottoman affairs. Both
countries were also aware of the need to protect their trade
routes to the Far East.

The Ottoman response to these uprisings was often harsh. Images
of 'barbarity' appeared on the front pages of the Western Press.
All this resulted in a change in the relationship between the
Ottoman government and her religious minorities, particularly
the Christians. Many leading Christians were suspected of being
spies working for Western powers. The Armenians in particular
were suspected of being on the side of Russia. Consequently, the
atmosphere of trust and tolerance towards the minorities that

ıd existed in the early centuries of Ottoman history began to change in the 19th Century. To some extent this was due to an Ottoman perception that European powers were meddling in Ottoman affairs.

While the situation was different in other parts of the Empire, for example Mesopotamia, the Levant and North Africa, Western involvement was equally evident here. This was particularly the case in Egypt when in 1805 Muhammad Ali, the Ottoman Governor in Cairo broke away from Istanbul and established an independent dynasty with the support of France. His aim was to become sole ruler of a reformed and modernised Egypt and the Levant.

Britain later became involved in Ottoman affairs during the First World War when the British Government encouraged Arab tribes in Arabia to rise up against their 'oppressive' Ottoman overlords. In return for this the Arabs were promised Arab independence.

The material in this book has been presented in chronological order with each chapter covering a particular historical period. Maps have also been included in the hope that they will make this complex history accessible to the general reader.

CHAPTER ONE
Turkic Tribes

Introduction

The Ottomans were a Turkic speaking people whose origins can be traced back to the Oghuz Turks who inhabited the Oghuz Yabgu State in the region of today's Kazakhstan. From about 900 AD, the various tribes that made up the Oghuz confederation began a gradual migration towards the west.

They travelled in small family or clan groups over a period of several centuries. Some took the mountainous route towards the Caspian Sea, on to Russia and even travelled as far as the Danube Delta. Others, for example the Seljuk tribe, migrated towards Iran and Iraq where they encountered Islam and subsequently became Muslim. The Seljuk tribes later established the Great Seljuk Empire.

The *Kayi* clan, also part of the Oghuz confederation, were the ancestors of the Ottomans. This clan migrated towards Anatolia, today's Turkey, where they finally settled and later founded the Ottoman Empire.

Today descendants of the various tribes that made up the Oghuz confederation can be found in Turkey, Turkmenistan, Azerbaijan and other Central Asian and Eastern European countries. Over time the word 'Oghuz' came to be replaced by the word *Turkmen* or *Turkomen.*

All these Turkic tribes were originally nomadic. In search of new pastures or fleeing aggressors they travelled across vast stretches of inhospitable desert and grasslands, making camp when necessary in tents that were quickly erected and just as speedily dismantled.

Speed was of the essence and they were famed for their short-legged sturdy horses that were as much part of the clan or family as were wives and children. When travelling at speed it was said that man and rider were almost indistinguishable. The riders were famed for being able to shoot arrows backwards at a speed of three every second and still hit their mark. The Turkic tribes were also formidable fighters and in recognition of this, those who became Muslim, were often referred to a *Ghazi*, an Islamic title of respect traditionally given to a powerful warrior.

Some features of nomadic life, such as skilled horsemanship and being constantly on the move, were retained by the later Seljuk and Ottoman peoples.

The Seljuks

Around the middle of the 10th Century the leader of the Seljuk clan broke away from the main Oghuz confederation and migrated towards Khurasan in Persia, which at that time was ruled by the Ghaznavids.

After originally fighting for the Ghaznavids, the Seljuks eventually overthrew their masters and established the Great Seljuk Empire, which stretched from the Eastern coast of the Mediterranean, across Central Asia to the borders with China.

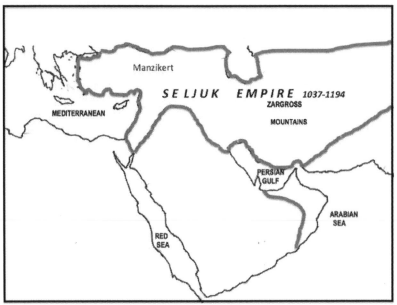

The Great Seljuk Empire lasted for approximately 160 years, from 1037 to 1194, and was a period that witnessed a coming together of Persian and Turkish cultures. Referred to as the Turko-Persian tradition, it combined Turkish and Persian languages, art, literature and culture.

One branch of the Seljuks, known as the *Sultanate of Rum*, began to encroach upon Christian Byzantine territory in Anatolia. The term *Rum* is taken from the Persian word for Roman and reflects their belief that the *Sultanate of Rum* was the legitimate successor to the Roman Byzantine Empire.

This was especially the case after 1071, when the Byzantines were beaten by the Seljuks at the Battle of Manzikert, a city close to Constantinople. Under their leader *Alp Arslan*, the Seljuks defeated the Byzantines and captured the Byzantine Emperor, Romanos Diogenes. After being held in captivity for several days, during which time he was well treated, peace was agreed conditional upon payment of a large ransom and a marriage contract between *Alp Arslan's* son and Romanos's daughter.

The Battle of Manzikert marked a watershed in the history of the region. With the defeat of the imperial army and the humiliation of the Emperor it was evident that the Byzantines could no longer defend their borders. This gave the Seljuks a perfect opportunity to move in and settle the region resulting in the gradual Turkification of Anatolia.

Following the Seljuk victory at Manzikert in 1071, *Alp Arslan* encouraged his generals to form their own principalities, known as *beyliks*, on previously held Byzantine territory. The *atabegs*, rulers of the *beyliks,* enjoyed considerable autonomy while at the same pledging loyalty to the Sultan.

The Seljuk Empire was at its greatest in terms of territory and power under *Alp Arslan's* son and successor *Malik Shah*, who ruled from 1072 to 1092. However, with *Malik Shah's* death the Seljuk Empire was divided among his various sons. As so often happens in history, this led to conflict and fragmentation.

The Crusades

It was the fear of Seljuk conquest, particularly of Constantinople, that prompted the Byzantine Emperor, Alexios I Komnenos, to appeal to Pope Urban II for military help. The Pope responded positively. In March 1095 he addressed a Council at Clermont in France calling on the Christian faithful to come to the defence of Eastern Christendom against the 'infidel' Seljuk Muslims, often referred to at the time as Saracens.

In August 1096 the armies of the First Crusade set off from Western Europe. Although Emperor Komnenos had asked for military aid to defend Byzantine territory from the Seljuks, the Pope had preached a crusade aimed at liberating Jerusalem. The prospect of freeing the Holy City from the infidel was far more appealing to the crowd than helping the Byzantines. Thousands of men, women and even children responded to the call and joined the crusading armies.

This Crusade was to be the first of four major Crusades that occurred between 1096 and 1204, all destined for Jerusalem. However, the Fourth Crusade in 1204 never did reach its destination. At the time the crusaders were short of money and became indebted to the Venetians who, for political reasons, persuaded the Western armies to sail for Jerusalem via Constantinople.

When the crusaders reached Constantinople they spent three days ransacking the city. They stole precious works of art, destroyed the valuable library, desecrated monasteries and churches and killed or raped the inhabitants. This shameful act by Western Christians against Eastern Christians is known as the Sack of Constantinople and further damaged an already difficult relationship between the Latin and Orthodox Christians.

In the aftermath, two leading Byzantine dynasties fled and established alternative empires in exile, one in Nicaea headed by the Paleologi dynasty and the other in Trabzon on the Black Sea coast under the Comneni family. The conquering Western crusaders founded a Latin Empire in Constantinople that was to last from 1204 to 1261. Not surprisingly, the inhabitants resented the Western presence, and particularly the imposition of a Western liturgy in their Eastern Orthodox churches.

After the departure of the Latin Christians the Byzantines returned to power. However, tension grew between the Paleologi and Comneni as both contended for the imperial throne. Political instability led the Empire into a slow decline and after 1204 the city of Constantinople never truly recovered its former glory, both factors that contributed to the ease with which the Ottoman Turks were able to conquer Constantinople in 1453.

The Mongol Invasion and decline of the Seljuks

In 1206, just two years after the Sack of Constantinople by the Western Crusaders, *Genghis Khan* was declared ruler of all the nomadic tribes of Mongolia. This was to be the beginning of the great Mongol Empire that lasted from 1206 to 1368. From its origins in the steppes of Central Asia the Empire expanded to cover an area from Central Europe to the Sea of Japan. It stretched northwards to Siberia, southwards into the Indian subcontinent and westwards to Anatolia, Iran and the Levant.

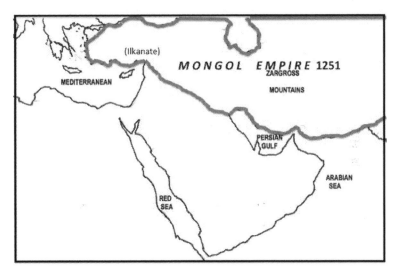

By the beginning of the 13th Century, during the reign of *Ogedei Khan,* son and successor to *Genghis Khan,* the Mongols had reached Anatolia. Initially the Seljuks offered friendship to the invaders in the hope of avoiding warfare. However, as Mongol influence increased to the point of the imposition of Mongol governors, the Seljuks began to rebel.

Consequently, the Mongols seized the city of Erzuram in today's Eastern Turkey and in June 1243 a major battle was fought between the Mongols and the Seljuks at *Kose Dag* in northeast Anatolia. Despite reinforcements from the Byzantine Empire of Trabzon, Western crusading mercenaries and a few Georgian nobles, the Mongols defeated the Seljuks. From this point on the various *beyliks* of Anatolia became vassals of the Mongols. This period of Mongol vassalage in the region is known as the *Ilkhanate* period, a time when the Mongols ruled territory that included Iran, Iraq, Georgia, Armenia and Anatolia.

By the beginning of the 14th Century the centralised power of the Sultanate of Rum had been destroyed leaving the numerous *beyliks*, which were nominally under Mongol rule, operating as autonomous principalities. The *Beylik* of the Osmanoglu Dynasty that was situated in *Sogut* in northwest Anatolia was later to found the Ottoman Empire.

Conclusion

The origins of the early Ottomans can be traced back to the *Kayi* clan of the Oghuz Yabgu State in the region of today's Kazakhstan. It was one clan among many others that over a period of several centuries, starting around 900 AD, migrated westwards. Those who passed through Muslim countries encountered Islam and subsequently became Muslim.

The *Seljuk* tribe became particularly powerful and by the middle of the 11th Century had overrun the *Ghaznavids* and founded the Great *Seljuk* Empire. One branch of the Empire, known as the *Sultanate of Rum* settled in Anatolia, today's Turkey.

The region of Anatolia was at that time part of the Byzantine, or Eastern Roman Empire and the *Seljuks* gradually encroached upon Byzantine territory. A battle ensued at Manzikert in 1071 but the Byzantines were severely defeated. It was this event that prompted the Emperor to appeal to the Pope in Rome for Western help to defend Eastern Christendom against the *Seljuks*.

The *Seljuks,* or Saracens, were in power at the time of the Crusades and were the main enemies of the crusaders. However, during the

Fourth Crusade in 1204, the Western crusaders turned against their fellow Christians in Constantinople sacking and desecrating the city.

The city of Constantinople never recovered its former glory. Two rival Byzantine Empires were established in Trabzon and Nicaea while a Latin Emperor ruled for some sixty years from Constantinople.

The centralised power of the *Seljuk Sultanate of Rum* was destroyed with the arrival of the Mongols in the middle of the 13th Century. Thereafter the Anatolian *beyliks* functioned as autonomous principalities under Mongol vassalage. By the middle of the 14th Century Mongol influence was in decline so giving the *beyliks* not only the freedom to rule themselves but also to compete with each other for regional power.

It was in this context that one *beylik* in particular rose to prominence. Known as the house of Osmanoglu it was later to found the Ottoman Empire.

Seljuk influence is still evident in today's Turkey. Apart from a town named Seljuk, which is situated very close to the ancient city of Ephesus, Seljuk mosques, monuments and architecture can be found dotted around the country.

CHAPTER TWO
Early Empire

Introduction

The founding of the Ottoman Empire is officially dated from 17 January 1299, which is when Osman Ghazi ben Ertugrul declared himself Sultan of the principality of *Sogut*. Osman inherited the *beyik* of *Sogut*, previously known as the Byzantine town of Thebasion, from his father Ertugrul in 1281. It was a time when the *Sultanate of Rum* was in decline and the Byzantine Empire was losing territory to rival Turkic tribes.

During his reign, which was to last until 1326, Osman extended his territory from *Sogut* towards the Byzantine cities of Bursa and Nicaea. His military prowess attracted many *ghazi* warriors and other migrant fighters from the region. He settled his forces on conquered land and in time Muslim traders, Islamic scholars and Sufi *dervishes* (ascetics) joined the nascent Muslim communities.

In recognition of his military skill Osman was given the title *Ghazi*. Although the term *ghazi* in Arabic can be interpreted in a pejorative sense, signifying an invading and plundering warrior, for the Ottomans at the time the title was one of respect. Osman was known as Sultan of the *Ghazis*, a title that subsequent Ottoman rulers also adopted.

Between 1299 and 1453 seven different Sultans ruled the House of Osman and during the same period the Ottomans brought most of Anatolia and large swathes of the Balkans into their sphere of influence. As vassals of the Sultan Muslim *beys* and Christian princes had to pay taxes and supply armies, both of which added to the increasing wealth and power of the Ottomans.

Finally, in 1453 Mehmet II, known as the Conqueror, captured Constantinople, the last bastion of Byzantine power, by that time a tiny Christian island surrounded by vast Muslim seas.

Osman I: foundation of Empire

As with many historical figures the early years of Osman's life is shrouded in mystery. There is also some confusion over his name. The accepted view is that he was named after *Uthman ibn Affan,* the third Caliph of the *Rashidun* (632-661CE), considered by many to be the period of 'pure' Islam. Some question the theory that Osman was named after Uthman because very few of Osman's other male relatives at the time were given Muslim names.

Osman was born in 1258 in Sogut, Anatolia. When his father Ertugrul died in around 1280, Osman inherited the lands around Sogut and the leadership of the *Kayi* clan of the *Oghuz* tribe. In 1299 he became Sultan, although considering the size of his domain at the time *emir* might have been a more accurate title. However, the discovery of an undated coin with the inscription "minted by Osman son of Ertugrul", supports both the historicity of a person named Ertugrul and also the status of Osman since the minting of coins was the prerogative of only a sovereign.

There is little historical data to explain why or how Osman came to dominate the neighbouring tribes. One way of counteracting the lack of historical evidence and in order to legitimise the rule of Osman as Sultan, the early Ottomans promoted the story of what is known as 'Osman's Dream'.

According to tradition, Osman had a dream while he was staying in the house of Sufi Sheik *Edebali,* a close friend of his father. *Edebali* was also a respected religious leader descending from the reputable *Banu Tamim* tribe of Arabia. In the dream Osman saw a crescent moon rise from the chest of the holy man and descend onto his own chest. Then a tree sprouted from his chest and the branches of the tree spread to give cover to numerous mountains and streams from which the people either drank or watered their crops and gardens.

When Osman later told *Edebali* about the dream the Sheik explained that it symbolised that Osman was destined for great imperial office. Furthermore, it was predicted that Osman would marry *Edebali's* daughter.

From this point *Edebali* became mentor to the Sultan, advising him in all aspects of governance that eventually came to influence Ottoman policy for centuries to come. *Edebali* also presented Osman with a *ghazi* sword. This same sword, known as the Sword of Osman, became the symbol of Ottoman power and was used at the Girding of the Sword Ceremony of all subsequent Sultans on the occasion of their enthronement.

Osman died in August 1326 at the age of 68. By this time, he had extended his territory to include the city of Eskisehir and also Bursa, which became strategically important in relation to the later conquest of Constantinople. Bursa also became the capital city of Osman's son and successor Orhan.

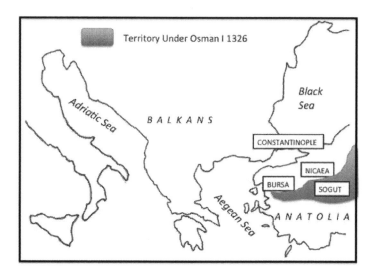

Orhan: a foot into Europe

Following his father's death Orhan ruled for over thirty years making him one of the longest reigning Sultans in Ottoman history. On his accession he put his brother Alaeddin in charge of the administration of the Empire making him in effect the first Grand Vizier. The root of the word *vizier* comes from the Arabic word *wazir,* meaning bearer of a burden and in this context the 'burden' was responsibility for the smooth running of the Empire. In time the role of the Grand Vizier became more formalised and also included responsibility for the military. Many of those who held the position were from Christian backgrounds and were second only in power to the Sultan.

Early in his reign Orhan secured the southern shores of Marmara, the small sea that connects the Black Sea with the Aegean. By this time trade between the Ottomans, the Byzantines and the various Italian maritime cities such as Venice and Genoa was commonplace. It was also usual for Ottoman mercenaries to fight for the Byzantines.

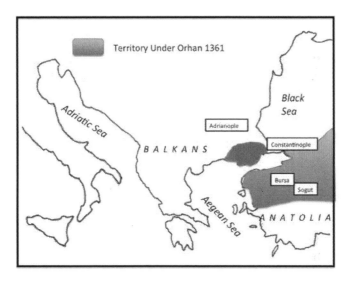

Orhan was also to benefit from the political instability of the Byzantines. As mentioned in the previous chapter, there was rivalry for the imperial throne between competing dynasties following the departure from Constantinople of the Latins in 1267. This eventually led to a series of civil wars and in 1354 a Byzantine rebel named Cantacuzenos appealed to Orhan for troops. Orhan responded favourably and consequently Ottoman troops, as opposed to individual mercenaries, crossed the small stretch of water that separates Asia from Europe in order to join the Byzantines.

Two years later, in March 1356, an earthquake struck Gallipoli destroying a nearby Greek castle that guarded the straits of the Dardanelles. Passing Ottoman troops heading towards Asia seized and occupied the ruins, so marking the first settlement of the Ottomans in Europe. And so began a steady stream of Turkish families, farmers and *beys* who crossed the Hellespont into Thrace in search of a better life, as migrants have done down the ages.

Not surprisingly intermarriage between the Ottomans and Byzantines also became commonplace at this time. Orhan, however, was the first Sultan to demand the hand of a Byzantine princess in order to cement relations between the two powers. His marriage to Princess Theodora became the first of many dynastic marriages between the Christian aristocracy of the Balkans and the Muslim House of Osman.

Janissaries

There is some difference of opinion as to when the Janissaries, *(jeni ceri)* meaning 'new troops' were formed. Orhan's son and successor Murad is often given credit for having founded the corps. However, while it is true that under Murad rules of recruitment and organisation became firmly established, the origins of the corps most likely date from Orhan's reign and particularly the contribution made by his brother Alaeddin who was in charge of military affairs.

In the early decades of Ottoman expansion the Sultan's armies were made up of volunteer *ghazis* and troops supplied by vassal states. The armies were disbanded after each period of action in a similar fashion to those in Western Europe. Alaeddin however, recognised the need for an army that would be permanently available to the Sultan and so he established the first standing army since the time of the Roman Empire. He also decided that as an incentive all 'new troops' would be put on regular pay.

While Orhan had succeeded in setting up a paid army he became alarmed at the growing arrogance of the recruits and eventually came to distrust them. His solution to the problem was quite radical. He ordered that all new recruits should be taken from the non-Muslim populations of the conquered territories. The policy was justified on the grounds that the Sultan had the right to enlist prisoners and slaves captured in war into his armies. Originally adult captives were enlisted but it was then thought that if these recruits were enlisted as young boys and trained under strict discipline by the Ottomans, they would make more committed and loyal troops. Essentially, non-Muslims who had been trained from an early age made better soldiers than freebooting *ghazis* and vassal troops.

The system of recruiting young boys became known as 'boy-tribute' or the *devsirme* system. The majority of the boys came from the Balkans and while the idea of taking children away from their families may sound cruel, most boys had opportunities under the Ottomans that would have been impossible in an impoverished Balkan village. All received an education and among those who were trained for palace duties, some went on to high positions, even that of Grand Vizier.

While the 'boy-tribute' probably began in an *ad hoc* manner under Orhan, the system was formalised by his successor Murad. Rules were then put into place regarding the frequency of recruitment, how the process should be conducted and by whom, including guidelines on which boys were, or were not, eligible. For example, Jews were exempt on religious grounds and where there was only one son in the family he was exempt on compassionate grounds.

The majority of the boys joined the Janissaries, the corps that became the feared crack troops of the Ottoman Empire. They received both a salary and a pension. Initially they were forbidden to grow beards or to marry but eventually these restrictions, along with others, were relaxed and by the early 17th Century corruption began to set in. In 1826 Sultan Mahmud II abolished the corps in favour of setting up a more modern army.

The 'boy-tribute' system went into decline during the 17th Century and was abolished finally during the reign of Ahmet III (1703-1730).

Sultan Orhan lived until the age of eighty, spending the last few years in retirement at Bursa. Shortly before his death his eldest son and heir Suleiman Pasha died following a fall from a horse. This left his second son, Murad, as successor to the Sultanate.

Between 1362 and 1389 Murad, the Third Sultan, succeeded in bringing large swathes of the Balkans either under direct Ottoman rule or under vassalage. He first conquered the Byzantine city of Adrianople in Thrace and renamed it Edirne. Edirne then became the capital of the Ottoman Empire and remained so until the fall of Constantinople in 1453.

However, the most significant military achievement of Murad's reign was his victory over the Serbs in June 1389 at the Battle of Kosovo, which is close to the modern city of Prishtina. Together with his sons Bayezid and Yakub, Murad led his army, which was more than twice the strength of his opponents, against Prince Lazar of Moravian Serbia and his allies including the Kingdom of Bosnia and the Knights of St John. There were heavy casualties on each side and both Sultan Murad and Prince Lazar lost their lives in the battle. The Serb forces were seriously depleted but the Ottomans were able to rally reinforcements from Anatolia. Faced with this reality the Serbs conceded defeat.

There are different accounts as to exactly how Murad met his death but a generally accepted view is that a Serbian warrior named Milos Obilic murdered him in his tent shortly after the battle. Murad's internal organs were buried in a corner of the battlefield where they remain to this day. The spot is known as *Meshed-i Hudavendigar* and continues to be revered by Muslims.

Serbs, on the other hand, refer to the location as Obilic in commemoration of their great war hero Milos Obilic who allegedly killed the Sultan. The Battle of Kosovo holds a key place in Serbian history in a way similar to that of the Battle of Hastings for the English. Both events impacted upon the subsequent tradition, culture and sense of identity of their peoples.

Apart from Murad's military achievements it was during his reign that the Ottomans made the transition from being a tribal confederation of Oghuz Turks into a recognisable Empire. As more Balkan states became Ottoman vassals, Ottoman influence grew. Non-Muslims living in Ottoman lands were promised protection and freedom of worship in exchange for payment of a special tax (*jizyah*), There were, however, certain restrictions placed upon them regarding permissible occupation and dress.

As already mentioned, it was during Murad's reign that both the Janissary Corps and the *devsirme*, or 'boy-tribute', became institutionalised. Murad also changed the system of land ownership. Officially the Sultan owned all Ottoman land and he would grant his governors and *spahis* (warrior horsemen) temporary land rights. The Byzantine feudal system, whereby landowners exacted two days' labour a week from their Serbian peasants, was replaced by a requirement for them to work just three days a year for their local governor, an arrangement that was far less onerous.

For administrative purposes Murad divided the empire into the two provinces of Anatolia (Asia Minor) and Rumelia (the Balkans). He organised a government system known as the *divan*, appointed *qadis* (religious judges) and invited Islamic teachers from Arabia to set up *madrassas* (religious schools).

Murad followed his father Orhan in that he also married a Christian Princess but this time it was to cement relations between the Ottomans and Bulgaria. Kera Tamara was the daughter of Bulgarian Emperor Ivan Alexander and despite marrying into the Ottoman dynasty she kept her Christian faith and campaigned for the rights of Christians living under Ottoman rule   for   the   remainder   of   her   life.

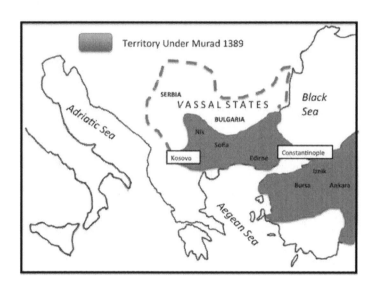

Conclusion

When Osman declared himself Sultan in 1299 he was merely the leader, or *Emir,* of the small principality of *Sogut.* When his grandson Murad died ninety years later in 1389 the tribe of Osman had grown into an empire that stretched from southern Anatolia to the banks of the Danube in the Balkans. It was an empire that incorporated territory in both Islamic Asia and Christian Europe.

From its capital in Edirne the Ottomans extended on two fronts: in southeast Anatolia where Muslim *beys* resisted Ottoman territorialism and in the Balkans where Christian Byzantine principalities gradually submitted to Ottoman vassalage. Constantinople, however, remained in Byzantine hands.

The vassal states were obliged to pay taxes and supply troops to the Sultan, so adding to Ottoman power and prestige. Under the 'boy-tribute' system a constant supply of young boys from the Balkans, who were trained for the elite Janissary Corps, strengthened the Ottoman fighting machine.

During the first decades of Ottoman rule relations with the Byzantines were fluid. Trade between the two powers was the norm and intermarriage was commonplace, particularly between ruling families.

The Byzantine Empire at this time was weak and unstable, a situation that led to a series of civil wars. In this context it was not unusual for Ottoman mercenaries to join either side in a civil war, in this case fighting alongside Byzantine forces. Equally Byzantine troops may be sent to Anatolia to fight alongside the Ottomans in their efforts to bring resistant *beyliks* and particularly the *Karamanids* of south central Anatolia into the Ottoman orbit of influence.

CHAPTER THREE

Bayezid 'The Thunderbolt'

Introduction

Bayezid and his brother Yacub fought alongside their father Murad at the famous Battle of Kosovo in 1389. When Murad was killed on the battlefield, 29 year old Bayezid immediately had his brother murdered, so securing the Sultanate for himself. This was to be the first recorded case of fratricide in Ottoman history.

Perhaps Bayezid acquired the nickname of 'Thunderbolt' because of the speed with which he seized the throne, or because of his lightning marches across Anatolia between the reluctant *beyliks* in the East and his Balkan vassals in the West. Whatever the reason for his name, it is generally accepted that he had a reputation for impulsive action and a fierce temper.

During his reign he extended Ottoman rule to include Bulgaria and northern Greece as well as most of Anatolia and he secured the vassalage of the Byzantine Emperor. But he antagonised the great Turco-Mongol warlord Timor, otherwise known as Tamerlane, an act that was to lead to his death.

Dynastic Marriages

In common with many other parts of the world dynastic marriages, or marriages of convenience, frequently took place in Ottoman history in order to cement loyalties between the Sultan and his vassals or potential enemies.

During the early period of the Ottoman conquest of the Balkans both Bayezid's father and grandfather had married Byzantine princesses. In around 1381, even before he became Sultan, Bayezid married Deviet Hatun, the daughter of Prince Suleyman, ruler of the Anatolian *beylik* of the Germiyanids. He hoped that this would secure his possession of Germiyanid territory.

In 1384 he married Maria Hatun, a Christian, who was daughter of the Count of Salona. Salona was a Latin crusader state that was established in Central Greece following the Fourth Crusade of 1204.

Following his victory at the Battle of Kosovo in 1389 Bayezid then married Despina Hatun, also a Christian, who was daughter of Prince Lazar of Serbia. This time he hoped that the marriage would lessen the risk of the Serbs attacking his Balkan provinces.

Believing that his Western territories were now secure he turned eastwards to concentrate on the illusive Anatolian be*yliks*. There he married Hafsa Hatun, daughter of the *Bey* of the Aydinids. By 1390, Bayezid controlled most of Western Anatolia. However, the most powerful and strategically important *beylik* of all, the Karamanids, still remained beyond his reach. The Ottomans had always known that in order to control the lucrative trade routes linking the Eastern Mediterranean with Central Asia they had to bring the Karamanids into the Ottoman orbit of control.

The Last Major Crusade

In 1390, just a year after defeating the Serbs at Kosovo, Bayezid laid siege to Constantinople, which was only lifted after the Emperor agreed to become an Ottoman vassal. This was to be the first of many sieges of the city until Constantinople finally fell to the Ottomans in 1453.

Three years after laying siege to Constantinople the Bulgarian city of Nicopolis, situated on the Danube, fell to the Ottomans.

The speed and success of the Ottoman advance across Europe caused Western European countries alarm. Hungary, now on the frontline between the Christian West and Islam, was particularly vulnerable. At the same time the Ottomans were seen as a threat by the maritime powers of Venice and Genoa who then controlled the sea-lanes of the Adriatic and Aegean.

It was against this background of increasing Ottoman expansion, coupled with the need to defend Christendom against Islam, that Pope Boniface IX proclaimed a crusade against the Turks. The initial aim was to liberate Nicopolis on the Danube and then to move on to relieve Constantinople.

In August, 1395 King Sigismund of Hungary sent a delegation to Paris with an appeal to King Charles VI of France for military help. A large number of French nobles, together with a fewer number of English, responded enthusiastically. They joined an allied army that included soldiers from the Holy Roman Empire, the Knights of St John, the Republics of Venice and Genoa, the Wallachia Knights and forces from the recently defeated Second Bulgaria Empire. King Sigismund and his Hungarian forces played a leading role.

The strength of the forces has been hotly disputed. However, taking account of logistics such as the time taken for troops to cross the River Danube and the ability of the surrounding countryside to supply food and fodder, it has been estimated that the European forces probably amounted to some 16,000 and the Ottomans about 15,000.

On 12th September 1396 the crusaders were in sight of the city of Nicopolis. They lay siege to the city for almost two weeks during which time many of the French knights drank heavily to relieve their boredom. When Bayezid's army was finally sighted the crusaders massacred some 1,000 Ottoman civilian hostages, an act that was later condemned by the Papacy and other European leaders.

On the morning of 25th September a fierce battle finally ensued. The outcome was a disaster for the crusader army. The majority were killed in battle with others taken captive, either for ransom or as conscripts for the Ottoman army. King Sigismund of Hungary and the Grand Master of the Knights of St John managed to escape by boat.

The different factions making up the allied forces blamed each other for the defeat. The French blamed the Hungarians for hesitancy and inaction while the Hungarians blamed the French knights for being drunk, unprepared and displaying rash, undisciplined behaviour on the battlefield.

This was to be the last attempt of a Western coalition to push back the Ottomans for many years. Consequently, Bayezid was able to cross to the northern banks of the Danube and seize more Hungarian territory unhindered.

Bayezid and Tamerlane

The Ottomans, together with the majority of independent Anatolian *beyliks,* traced their origins to the Turkic migrations of the 10th Century. Other Anatolian *beyliks* traced their ancestry to the Mongol Ilkhanate of the 13th Century that was founded by the great Genghis Khan (see Chapter One)

At the end of 13th Century Timor (Tamerlane), who was the grandson of Genghis Khan, began annexing Anatolian territory as part of his wider conquest of the Levant. Some of this territory was under the vassalage of Bayezid and this naturally brought Timor and Bayezid into conflict.

Those *beyliks* that now found themselves conquered by Timor swore allegiance to him despite the fact that they had previously been vassals of Bayezid. This was something that the Sultan, fresh from his conquests in the Balkans and in a confident and triumphant mood, could not accept

Tension between the two leaders finally led to open warfare. On 20th September 1402 the Timurids and the Ottomans, who were joined by heavily armed Serbs and Wallachian knights, confronted each other at the Battle of Ankara.

Prior to engagement Timor diverted the sole water supply in the area, leaving the Ottomans with no water. Bayezid was severely defeated, partly because his men were exhausted and thirsty and also because so many of his Anatolian vassals switched sides and joined Timor. Again statistics are disputed but it is thought that each side suffered around 40,000 to 50,000 casualties.

Bayezid managed to escape but was quickly captured by Timor's men. There are various accounts of the Sultan's captivity, the subject of which has been recreated by Western painters, writers and composers, for example, Christopher Marlowe's play *Tamburlaine the Great* and Vivaldi's *Bajazet*. Much of this material has been embellished, for example portraying Bayezid held captive in cage that Timor carried with him on campaign while his Serbian wife was forced to serve naked at Timor's court.

The Ottoman Interregnum

Bayezid died in captivity in March 1403, less than a year after his defeat by Timor at Ankara. His son Mustafa Celebi, who was captured alongside his father, was released from Samarkand in 1405. Four of Bayezid's other sons, Suleyman, Isa, Mehmet and Musa, managed to escape but immediately started fighting among themselves over who should succeed as Sultan.

It was not until 1413, ten years after the death of Bayezid that Mehmet, known as Mehmet I, managed to secure the throne so ending a decade of political instability referred to as the Ottoman Interregnum. During this same period many of the Anatolian *beyliks* rebelled against Ottoman rule and regained their independence.

Even after the enthronement of Mehmet the Sultanate was not secure. His brother Mustafa, who had been held captive by Timor in Samarkand, reappeared. His surprise appearance has led some to suggest that he might have been an imposter. This 'Mustafa' demanded that Mehmet divide the empire between them. When Mehmet refused 'Mustafa' resorted to war but was easily defeated.

Despite having lost parts of Anatolia, Mehmet managed to secure the vassalage of Mircea and Wallachia in the Balkans. As was traditional at the time, the three sons of Mircea were sent to the Ottoman court as hostages in order to ensure their father's loyalty to the Sultan. One of these sons happened to be Vlad Drakul, later known as 'Vlad the Impaler', on account of his favoured use of impalement as a form of execution for his enemies. He is popularly known in Western literature and cinema as the vampire Count Dracula of Transylvania.

Conclusion

Bayezid ruled for approximately fourteen turbulent years. His reign began under murky circumstances surrounding the death of his elder brother, an event that enabled him to secure the throne for himself. In common with other leaders of the time he married the daughters of both his Christian and Muslim vassals believing that this would guarantee their loyalty.

Probably his greatest achievement was his victory in 1396 at the Battle of Nicopolis when his forces pushed back an allied Christian army under the leadership of King Sigismund of Hungary. However, throughout his reign he antagonised the independent-minded Anatolian *beyliks,* particularly the powerful Karamanids.

Bayezid's downfall came when Timor, grandson of the great Mongol leader Genghis Khan, began a campaign of conquest across the Levant. In the process several of Bayezid's Anatolian vassals were seized by Timor. Indignant and over-confident, Bayezid confronted Timor and this resulted in a military conflict at the Battle of Ankara in 1402. He was severely defeated, however, partly because many of his disgruntled vassals changed sides and joined Timor's forces.

Bayezid's death left the Ottomans with no ruler and ten years of political and social instability followed, known as the Ottoman Interregnum. The Interregnum is viewed as something of a watershed in Ottoman history since it marks the end of an initial period of growth and expansion.

The early expansion into the Balkans naturally resulted in confrontation between Christendom and Islam. The first major conflict had happened during the crusading period of the 11th and

12th Centuries between the predominantly French crusading forces and the Seljuk Turks (see Chapter One). Once more, in the 14th Century, an allied army of 'crusaders' under King Sigismund of Hungary attempted to fight back the Ottomans at the Battle of Nicolopolis. The Westerners were defeated and the front line of the Ottoman Empire moved further into Europe.

Today Hungary still sees herself on the frontline between the Christian West and Islam. In the light of her history it is perhaps not surprising that Hungary views the current mass migration of Syrian refugees across her borders, the majority of whom are Muslim, as a threat to Western civilisation and Christian identity. The outworking of this deep-seated fear of Islam is now manifesting itself with the building of fences and walls in order to keep Europe safe from what is perceived as an Islamic threat.

CHAPTER FOUR

Conquest of Constantinople

Introduction

In the West we speak of the Fall of Constantinople whereas Ottoman historians refer to the Conquest of Constantinople. Whether understood as the 'fall' or 'conquest', the fact is that the city passed from Byzantine to Ottoman rule on 29th May, 1453 and the event is a watershed in European history in that it marks the final collapse of the Byzantine Empire.

At the time Christians across Europe were traumatised by the realisation that Constantinople, a city founded by Constantine, the first Christian Emperor, as capital of the Roman Empire, had fallen to the Turks. The cultural and religious repercussions were felt from Moscow in the East to Amsterdam in the West and the consequent mass migration of scholars fleeing Ottoman held territories contributed towards the unfolding of the Renaissance in Western Europe.

From the perspective of the Ottomans the conquest was the culmination of a long-held dream. They viewed Constantinople, capital of the Roman Empire and its successor, the Eastern Roman or Byzantine Empire, as the 'Second Rome', the first being Ancient Rome. Following the conquest, the Ottoman Sultan Mehmet the Conqueror declared himself 'Caesar of [the Third] Rome' seeing himself in a direct line of succession from the Caesars of Ancient Rome.

Mehmet II, the Conqueror

Mehmet was born in Edirne in March 1432. When he was eleven years old he was sent by his father Murad II to Amasya in Northern Anatolia to study under the influential scholar *Akshamsaddin* who is also famed for having discovered the tomb of Abu Ayyub al-Ansari, companion and standard bearer of Prophet Muhammad.

Apart from following classical Islamic studies plus science and medicine, Mehmet was also introduced to aspects of Sufism, which is a mystical dimension of Islam. When his father died after an illness in the winter of 1450-1451, Mehmet succeeded to the throne as Mehmet II. He was just 19 years old.

Mehmet was not popular at the time and in order to ingratiate himself with his troops he offered them a donation. From that time on, all succeeding Sultans distributed a donation to their troops when they ascended to the throne.

Within a year of becoming Sultan, Mehmet spoke of his ambition to conquer Constantinople. The proposal was not well received. Apart from many previous failed attempts to take the city, the timing seemed inappropriate since his father had established good relations with the Byzantines.

However, Mehmet reminded those who opposed him that although the city might appear impregnable because it was protected on three sides by water and was surrounded by enormous fortifications, it was a shell of its former self. All that remained within its walls were vineyards and empty houses and churches, many of which were in ruins. Where streets previously teemed with life they were now used for small-scale farming. In fact, the city had never fully recovered from its desecration by Western crusaders in 1204.

The population of Constantinople in 1453 was small, with perhaps fewer than five thousand men capable of fighting. Any attempt to take the city, however, would not be without risk. There was always the danger that an attack would provoke a counter attack by the many Christian states that would no doubt come to the aid of the Byzantines.

In the event Byzantine appeals to the West turned out to be fruitless. Venice, Genoa and Ragusa (today's Dubrovnik) were too dependent upon Ottoman trade to risk upsetting their trade partners. Also both the Pope and Holy Roman Emperor had more pressing concerns nearer home. Furthermore, relations between the Papacy and Byzantines had been strained ever since the Schism of 1054 that had divided the Church into the Eastern Orthodox and Western Catholic branches.

Preparations for the Siege

At the beginning of 1452, in preparation for the siege, Mehmet built a castle known as *Rumeli Hisar* (the Strait Blocker) on the European side of the Bosporus right opposite another castle that had previously been built on the Asian side by Bayezid. This gave Mehmet complete control of the narrow strip of water that was so vital for ships carrying goods to the city.

The Byzantines feared an immanent attack. In desperation Emperor Constantine XI appealed to the Pope for aid in exchange for union under the Papacy between the Eastern and Western churches. But there was fierce opposition to such a proposal among both the clergy and laity of the Byzantine church, many who still held bitter memories of the treatment they received at the hands of the Latin crusaders in 1204.

Even had there been no opposition to the union from the Byzantines, the Pope's position at the time was weak and he was in no position to raise troops in any great number. While no major Western force came to the aid of the Byzantines certain individuals did, one being the Genoese soldier Giovanni Giustiniani who arrived with 700 men. Giustiniani died in battle but it is said that his bravery so impressed Mehmet that he would have given anything to have the soldier fight on the side of the Ottomans.

When appeals to the West failed the Emperor tried a last attempt to appease the Sultan with an offer of gifts. Mehmet responded by executing Constantine's ambassador so giving a clear indication that all diplomatic relations were severed.

The Byzantine army numbered about 7,000 men including foreign fighters and monks. The population of the city, including refugees from the surrounding area, was probably less than 50,000. Everyone became involved in the defence of the city by repairing walls, guarding posts, collecting and distributing food and even melting down silver from churches in order to pay foreign troops.

Perhaps the most effective tactic that the Byzantines employed was the use of a huge defensive chain that was mounted on floating logs. It was strung across the mouth of the harbour in order to stop Turkish ships getting close to the city's walls.

The Ottomans had a much larger force of between 50,000 and 80,000 men. It is estimated that between 5,000 and 10,000 of these were Janissaries, the Sultan's elite corps (see Chapter Two). Mehmet was also joined by a contingency of Serbian cavalry numbering around 1,500.

The Ottoman navy was also far larger than that of the Byzantines who could only muster around 30 ships. Mehmet's navy numbered 126 ships including six large galleys, 25 smaller galleys, 25 rowing boats and some 20 horse transports.

Apart from sheer numerical force, Mehmet had another great advantage. For some time, the Ottomans had been able to caste cannons. However, in preparation for this siege a Hungarian named Orban was commissioned to design a cannon that broke new ground in terms of both size and power. Named 'Basilica', it was 26 feet long and was able to hurl a 600 lb. stone ball over a distance of a mile. It took three hours to reload and needed a crew of 60 oxen and 400 men to transport it overland.

The Siege

Before the siege began Mehmet forced two minor Byzantine fortresses on the Bosporus into submission so clearing the way of any opposition. Then on Monday 2nd April, just after Easter, the Ottoman army made camp on the landside around the city walls. On 5th April Mehmet arrived with his personal troops while the defenders made their last desperate attempts to strengthen the fortifications from the inside.

On 6th April the first cannon ball smashed into the walls. It is said that the noise was so loud that it caused women to faint. The initial damage was repaired by the Byzantines overnight. This was to be a pattern that continued for weeks. In the meantime, the defensive chain plus the use of Byzantine 'Greek Fire', which was a form of napalm, succeeded in keeping the Ottomans out of the harbour.

As the weeks passed the Ottomans tried different tactics. They tunnelled under the fortifications and they built a road of greased logs so that they could transport their enormous cannons and ships overland to the North side of the Golden Horn.

On 25th May, some seven weeks into the siege, Mehmet sent an ambassador to Constantinople offering to raise the siege provided the Emperor hand over the city. Mehmet further promised that all inhabitants would be allowed safe passage to leave with all their possessions. He further promised that those who chose to stay would be unharmed. Constantine XI responded by offering to pay tribute to the Sultan but he could not and would not surrender the city.

At this point Mehmet consulted with his senior council. While a minority advised retreat the majority, mainly the younger *beys,* voted for an all-out attack.

The Final Assault

Preparations began on Sunday 26th May and continued until midnight on the 27th when the Ottoman camp fell into an eerie silence. The following day was spent in prayer and fasting while Mehmet toured the camp encouraging his men and reminding them of their duties. He also promised the customary booty that they were entitled to under Koranic law whenever a city refused to surrender.

Within the city walls Constantine urged the people to be brave. But the omens were not good. Icons were said to weep tears and records state that a statue of the Virgin Mary that was being carried in a religious procession slipped into the mud and could not be raised.

On the eve of the assault the people flocked to the great Church of the Hagia Sophia where Greeks and Catalans, Catholic and Orthodox came together for Holy Communion regardless of whether they normally followed the Greek or Latin rite. At this point all doctrinal differences were put aside in the face of a common enemy.

Before dawn, in the early hours of Wednesday 29th May, the attack began. Mehmet sent his irregular troops in first. Many were Christian slaves or subjects of his vassal states. There were Slavs, Hungarians, Italians and Greeks as well as Kurds and Turks from Anatolia. All were forced on with whips and instantly executed if they tried to escape. After two relentless hours the Anatolian infantry joined the fray and began climbing the walls. Finally came Mehmet's elite corps, the Janissaries, marching to the beat of their deafening drums, pipes and clash of symbols.

Hundreds were crushed to death or fell from ladders. Eventually, through sheer numerical strength, the Ottomans managed to get across the outer wall and then it was just a matter of time before the Ottoman flag was seen flying from a tower inside the city. Emperor Constantine fought bravely to the end but died in the midst of bitter hand-to-hand fighting.

The following day the Sultan rode into the city. Despite his promise to allow his troops the customary three days looting, he called a stop to all killing, plunder and desecration before the time was up. It seems that he was sickened by what he witnessed. Apart from the killing and maiming he was shocked to find the city in such a sorry state.

Eyewitness accounts state that he was so saddened by what he saw that tears came to his eyes. What had been one of the most beautiful cities in the world was now reduced to ruins. Furthermore, there was little left to plunder because the Latin Crusaders had taken the best of the treasure during the Fourth Crusade two hundred years earlier.

The Aftermath

Mehmet the Conqueror saw himself as the rightful successor to the Byzantine Emperor. He believed that he was Caesar of the Third Rome and it was his intention to restore the city to its former glory.

His first act was to declare that all surviving inhabitants who were in hiding had nothing to fear. Everyone, including those who had fled the city, could return unharmed to their homes. If homes had been damaged they would be restored.

He then converted the Byzantine Church of the Hagia Sophia into a mosque. He removed the bells, altar and iconostasis and replaced the cross with four minarets. He then installed a *mihrab*, which is a niche in the wall indicating the direction of Mecca towards which Muslims direct their prayer, and a *minbar*, or pulpit. The Byzantine mosaics were plastered over.

Of the remaining Christian churches, some thirty-six were preserved. The young Sultan realised that if he were to maintain the loyalty of his Greek subjects he must protect and support the Orthodox Church. He sought out the philosopher and scholar Gennadius Scolarius who was well known for his opposition to Rome and proposals for Union. Mehmet had Gennadius consecrated by the Archbishop of Heraclea as the new Patriarch hoping that by appointing a staunch Greek, who was fiercely anti-Rome, he would avert the possibility of another Western crusade.

The Chief Rabbi was called from Jerusalem in order to minister to the Jewish population and the Armenian Patriarch was transferred from Bursa. These religious minority communities were known as *millets* and were self-governed by their religious leaders under the *dhimmi* system which allowed freedom of worship and other protection on payment of a special *jizya,* or poll tax.

While Greek scholars and intellectuals had been leaving the city in the decades prior to 1453, after the fall of the city their number multiplied. Most of these intellectuals fled to Italy where their scholarship contributed to the European Renaissance.

However, a large number of Greek, Venetian and Genoese traders remained and apart from becoming extremely wealthy and influential, some were given key positions in the Sultan's household and government.

In order to help repopulate Constantinople Mehmet freed his slaves and provided them with homes and land. As he travelled around his Empire, conquering new territory, he sent captured slaves back to Constantinople. He also relocated whole communities from parts of Anatolia to the capital in his effort to create a thriving multi-religious and multi-ethnic city worthy of the title of the Third Rome.

Conclusion

The early centuries of Ottoman history are marked by expansion into the Balkans and a continuing effort to subdue and unite the various Anatolian *beyliks*. During this time the Byzantines were not only losing their vassals in the Balkans to the Ottomans but their capital city of Constantinople was becoming increasingly isolated and in danger of falling to the Turks.

The arrival of the Mongols, the capture of Bayezid and the Ottoman Interregnum gave the Byzantines something of a breathing space from the fear of losing their capital. Expectations of the young Mehmet were not high on his accession but after the conquest of Constantinople he became a hero, known as 'the Conqueror'.

While he earned the accolade of 'Conqueror' he also proved himself magnanimous in victory and treated his Greek citizens well. More significantly however he adopted a policy of repopulating a city that would be multi-cultural and multi-faith. He had the foresight to realise that if Constantinople was to succeed as the capital of an expanding Ottoman Empire it needed, above all, to be a successful centre for trade. For this he needed the expertise of the Greek sailors, Jewish bankers and Genoese traders.

For Christians across Europe the Fall of Constantinople was a shock. Naughty children would be told to fear 'the Turk' but more importantly Western European rulers realised that Christendom and their civilisation was under threat.

There is no doubt that the year 1453 and the fall of the Byzantine Empire marked a turning point in European history that is seen most clearly in the changing relationships between the Christian West and Ottoman East. It is also reflected in establishment of formal diplomatic relations between the Ottomans and several Western states as well as the Papacy.

The Conquest of Constantinople, increasingly known as Istanbul after 1453, also changed the balance of power in the region. Apart from the Muslim conquest of Andalusia in the 8th Century, this was the first time in European history that a major Muslim power had entered the European stage and it was a power that could no longer be ignored.

CHAPTER FIVE
Suleiman the Magnificent

Introduction

By the end of Mehmet II's reign in 1481 the Ottomans had conquered the whole of the Byzantine Empire, including the Peloponnese and Greek islands of the Aegean. Between 1481 and the accession of Suleiman the Magnificent in 1520, the Ottomans continued with their policy of consolidation in Anatolia and they further expanded their territory into the Levant, Arabia and Egypt. During this same period, however, new tensions arose on the Eastern border with the Persian Safavids.

Mehmet's eldest son, Bayezid II, succeeded his father in 1481 but another brother, Cem also claimed the throne. In his attempt to seize the Sultanate Cem sought military help from the Mamluks of Egypt. But the plan failed and Cem was forced to seek the protection of the Knights of St John whose headquarters at that time were on the island of Rhodes. The Knights only granted Cem refuge under condition that the Sultan paid for the pretender's upkeep. Cem was later handed over to Pope Innocent VIII and he remained in Papal custody until his death, at just 35 years of age, in 1495.

Throughout Cem's period of exile Bayezid II paid for his younger brother's upkeep. He was well treated and well-liked by his hosts and was a particular favourite of the Borgia Pope, Alexander VI. But he was virtually a prisoner, being denied the right to return home on the grounds that he would present a threat to the throne. Finally, four years after his death, Cem's body was returned to his homeland for a burial befitting his status. Cem's exile was a departure from the normal Ottoman practise of fratricide whereby younger brothers who were considered a threat to the throne would have been murdered.

Bayezid II's rule lasted until May 1512. Apart from his early struggles with Cem and the on-going process of consolidation, he is remembered for his open policy towards the Jews. In 1492, when King Ferdinand and Queen Isabella expelled all Jews from

Spain, the Sultan sent ships from the Ottoman Navy to help with the evacuation and resettlement of Jews in Ottoman lands. Bayezid II claimed that the Spanish monarchy's loss was the Ottoman's gain because his new citizens would bring many skills that would be of benefit to his Empire. Spanish Jews, for example, established the first printing press in Istanbul in 1493.

Bayezid II's final years were marked by a succession struggle between his two sons Selim and Ahmet. Selim, the younger of the two, seized the throne with the help of the Janissaries and it is believed that he promptly arranged the death of Ahmet and anyone else, including his nephews, who might challenge the succession.

Known as Selim I, or the Grim on account of his stern and implacable manner, he ruled from 1512 to 1520. During these eight years he conquered the Mamluk Sultanate of Egypt, which included the Levant, the Hejaz and Egypt itself. Significantly, by bringing the Hejaz into the Ottoman Empire, Selim became the defender of the Holy Cities of Mecca and Medina. From this time on, until the dissolution of the Empire in 1923, the Ottomans were to be the official guardians of the two most holy cities in Islam. Apart from the obvious prestige that this brought, the Ottomans also gained the lucrative trade connected with Muslim pilgrimage to Mecca for the annual *Hajj*.

As successor to the Mamluks, the Ottomans also inherited the *Caliphate.* Strictly speaking there can be only one *Caliphate* in the Muslim world. Traditionally the title *Caliph*, being leader of all Muslims, dates back to the time of the Prophet Muhammad. Following the *Rashidun,* (period of the first four *Caliphs*) the *Caliphate* passed on through the *Umayyad* and *Abbasid* periods with capitals in Damascus and Baghdad respectively. When the Mongols conquered the *Abbasids* in 1258 the *Caliphate* was transferred to the Mamluks in Egypt.

With the defeat of the Egyptians in 1517 the Ottomans inherited the *Caliphate,* which it held until 1923 when the Empire was finally dissolved. When the Ottoman Empire capitulated following the First World War, the Islamic world also lost its *Caliphate,* its centre of Islamic authority, even if that authority was only symbolic. Since that time there has been a vacuum in the Muslim world into which contenders for the *Caliphate* are emerging. At the time of writing one group, calling themselves the 'Islamic State', or *Daesh*, are claiming to be the legitimate inheritors of the *Caliphate* to which Muslims worldwide owe allegiance. (See my publication *Making Sense of Militant Islam*)

Suleiman the Magnificent

Suleiman, known as the Magnificent in the West, was more commonly called Suleiman the Lawgiver (*Kanuni*) by the Ottomans. It is said that he referred to himself as Suleiman II in deference to the first Suleiman (Solomon) of the Hebrew Scriptures. He was probably the greatest of all Ottoman Sultans, being both admired and feared by European and Asian rulers as well as his own subjects. He was known for his magnanimity towards his enemies while at the same time ruling his own people with an iron fist.

His long reign of 46 years coincided with other significant world rulers, including Charles V, Holy Roman Emperor; Francis I, King of France; Henry VIII and Elizabeth I, Monarchs of England; Babur, Mughal Emperor of India; Ismail I, Shah of Persia and Ivan the Terrible, Tsar of Russia. He regularly received diplomatic envoys from these monarchs that frequently included requests for help. For example, Francis I of France once appealed to the Sultan for help when he was imprisoned by Charles V and Babur the Mughal Emperor appealed for arms and military expertise for his war against the Persians.

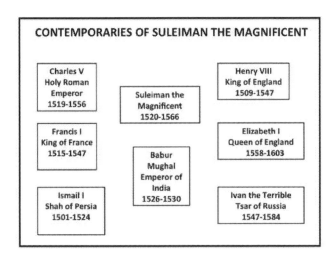

CONTEMPORARIES OF SULEIMAN THE MAGNIFICENT

Charles V
Holy Roman
Emperor
1519-1556

Suleiman the
Magnificent
1520-1566

Henry VIII
King of England
1509-1547

Francis I
King of France
1515-1547

Babur
Mughal
Emperor of
India
1526-1530

Elizabeth I
Queen of England
1558-1603

Ismail I
Shah of Persia
1501-1524

Ivan the Terrible
Tsar of Russia
1547-1584

Suleiman came to the throne at the age of 26 following the unexpected death of his father, probably from cancer. Since he had no brothers his succession proceeded smoothly, avoiding the distressful murder of any male siblings as so often happened under the practice of fratricide.

On 30th September, 1520 Suleiman was escorted to Eyup, the mosque and tomb that marked the burial place of Eyup Ensari, said to be the standard bearer of the Prophet Muhammad. Eyup had lost his life during the first Arab siege of Constantinople in 676 AD and his burial place was discovered during the siege of Constantinople in 1453. Mehmet II had built a mosque and tomb on the site, which then became the third most holy city for Ottomans after Mecca and Jerusalem. Eyup also became the traditional venue for the 'Girding of the Sword' ceremony whereby all Ottoman Sultans received the great sword of their ancestor warrior and founder, Osman Ghazi.

Suleiman marked his accession with the traditional donation of money to his troops, said to be more generous than that of his father. He lifted the trade sanctions on the Persians that his father had imposed, a move that proved popular with many of his subjects, particularly the silk merchants. He also freed leading Egyptian intellectuals who had been taken prisoner during the wars with the Mamluks. At the same time, he carried out executions of those of his own subjects who he considered to be corrupt or criminal.

Belgrade

Within a year of his accession Suleiman sent an envoy to Hungary offering to suspend raids in exchange for tribute. The offer was declined but fearing an Ottoman attack the Hungarians sent their own envoy to Worms in Germany where Charles V, Holy Roman Emperor, was holding a diet (imperial council). The Hungarians were hoping to gain military support from the princes of the Empire but at that particular diet, in 1521, Charles V was more concerned with what he perceived as a far greater threat: the heretic Martin Luther and growing Protestant dissent that threatened the survival of his Empire.

When the Hungarians rejected Suleiman's offer the Sultan lost no time in advancing on Belgrade, which was a dependency of Hungary and after a siege lasting just one week he was able to take the city with little difficulty. The capture of Belgrade was a major triumph for the Ottomans. Located in modern Serbia at the confluence of the Rivers Sava and Danube it provided a perfect launching pad for further incursions into Western Europe.

Because the city refused the offer of peace in exchange for tribute, Belgrade was razed and the majority of its Orthodox Christian population were deported to Istanbul. Belgrade became the second largest city of Ottoman Europe after Istanbul and apart from short periods of rebellion it remained under the Ottomans until Serbia gained independence in 1882.

Knights of St John

The Military Order of the Knights of St John, also known as the Knights Hospitaller, was founded in Jerusalem in 1113 shortly after the First Crusade. In 1291 the Mamluks of Egypt expelled the Crusaders from the Holy Land and the Knights sought refuge on the island of Cyprus. In 1309, desiring their own independent territory, they seized the island of Rhodes from the Byzantines and established an independent ecclesiastical territory answering directly to the Pope.

Once on Rhodes the Knights built an enormous fortress. They organised themselves into units, or *tongues*, according to their language or nationality. Each unit was allocated a specific responsibility within the Order and was also required to defend a particular portion of the fortified walls when under attack. The most powerful position, that of Grand Master, always went to a Frenchman. The Knights owned many ships and were also expected to protect and defend Christians travelling to the Holy Land.

Nevertheless, Suleiman viewed their presence in Ottoman seas as a threat to both the Ottoman grain trade with Egypt and also the safety of Muslim pilgrims who travelled by sea each year to Mecca. The Knights frequently attacked Ottoman vessels, took prisoners and operated a lucrative slave trade.

In 1522 Suleiman decided that it was time to evict the Knights from Rhodes. On the 26th June an invasion force of 400 ships, under the command of Mustafa Pasha, sailed the short distance from mainland Anatolia to Rhodes. Suleiman followed a few days later with an army estimated to be between 100,000 and 200,000 men. The defending army consisted of just 7,500 men including some 700 Knights and 500 archers.

The Knights put up a brave defence, helped by their massive fortifications but the hoped for relief forces failed to arrive; after five months both sides had suffered huge losses and were exhausted. Suleiman offered the Knights and inhabitants peace and freedom if they surrendered the island. Under pressure from the population the Knights finally agreed, a truce was declared and on 22nd December, 1522 the Knights surrendered.

Suleiman's terms were generous. The Knights were given twelve days to prepare for their departure and they were permitted to take everything, including weapons, icons and other valuables with them. The people were given the choice as to whether to leave or to stay. Those who remained would be free from Ottoman taxation for five years and word was given that no church should be desecrated or turned into a mosque.

On 1st January, 1523 the Knights, in full battle armour and accompanied by drums and flying banners, boarded ships provided by Suleiman and sailed for Crete. The Grand Master spent several years travelling across Western Europe in search of a new home until finally, in 1530, Emperor Charles V offered them the island of Malta in exchange for an annual payment of one Maltese falcon.

Although the Knights were now beyond Ottoman seas they still presented a thorn in the side of Suleiman. With the help of the Spanish they constantly attacked Ottoman ships sailing between Istanbul and North Africa, seizing cargo and taking captives, many of them pilgrims, for sale as slaves.

In 1565, more than thirty years after the Knights had settled on Malta, Suleiman once more decided to try and rid the Mediterranean of their presence. He sent a naval force under the command of Lala Mustafa Pasha, together with the feared Admiral Dragut, to take the island. The actual number of ships and combatants on both sides has always been disputed but what is not in dispute is that the Ottoman forces far outweighed those of the Knights.

The Ottomans laid siege to the island for over three months, from 18th May to 11th September. During this time the Knights, aided by around 2,000 foot soldiers and some 400 Maltese men, women and children put up a fierce defence. On 7th September the Spanish General Don Garcia landed at St Paul's Bay with reinforcements and just a few days later the Ottoman ships sailed away.

Malta remained the home of the Knights of St John until they were evicted by Napoleon in 1798.

Hungary

With the eviction of the Knights from Rhodes in 1523 the Eastern Mediterranean was freed from piracy and Suleiman was able to turn his attention once more to Europe. In August 1526 he advanced with his troops from Belgrade to the Hungarian town of Mohacs, situated on the right bank of the Danube. Here he encountered an allied army under the leadership of 20 year old

King Louis II of Hungary. The allies consisted of troops from Hungary, Croatia, Bohemia, Bavaria, Poland, The Papal States and the Holy Roman Empire. Despite this impressive coalition the allies were defeated and large swathes of Hungary came under Ottoman rule. Other areas came under the Habsburg Monarchy or the Kingdom of Transylvania.

The Battle of Mohacs was a major turning point in the history of Europe marking the transition from the various Ottoman-Hungarian Wars to the Ottoman-Habsburg Wars that were to continue until the outbreak of World War I.

Siege of Vienna 1529

Having defeated the Hungarians at Mohacs it was only a matter of time before Suleiman decided on his next and most ambitious European campaign; the capture of Vienna.

On 10th May 1529, almost three years after Mohacs, he left Istanbul at the head of an army estimated at between 150,000 and 200,000 men. As he crossed the Balkans into Europe his vassal armies, including troops from Moldavia, Belgrade and Ottoman Hungary, joined the main force swelling the numbers up to a possible 300,000.

Once into Bulgaria the troops encountered their first major obstacle. The Balkan rains were heavier than normal and had caused severe flooding. The great cannons got bogged down in mud, camels drowned and men became sick.

Despite the difficult journey and many losses Suleiman arrived at Mohacs on 18th August when he was joined by the cavalry forces of John Zapolya, King of Ottoman Hungary. Suleiman and Zapolya then marched together towards Vienna capturing the city of Buda, modern Budapest, along the way.

As the Ottomans approached Vienna the citizens did what they could to reinforce the walls. They were helped by 70 year old Nicholas, Count of Salm, a German officer renowned for his military skills.

Suleiman arrived at the walls of Vienna at the end of September. He had lost artillery and his forces were depleted through death and sickness. Food was short and morale low. On 11ᵗʰ October a further heavy downpour of rain added to the miseries of the Ottoman troops. The Janissaries complained at the lack of progress and on 12ᵗʰ October Suleiman called a council to discuss the situation. On 15ᵗʰ October he gave the order to retreat.

Suleiman died in 1566 while on campaign in Hungary. He was 71 years of age.

Conclusion

The long reign of Suleiman the Magnificent, which lasted for over forty years, is considered to be the golden age of Ottoman History. Between 1520 and 1566 he extended the empire into Europe as far as Budapest, in the East to Baghdad and the Caspian Sea, in the south as far as Yemen and the West to Algeria.

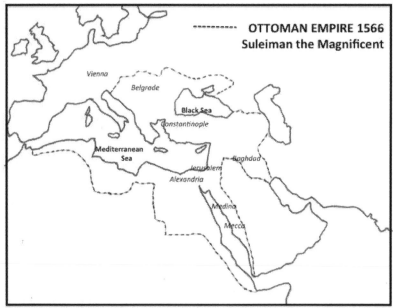

His navy was the most powerful in the Eastern Mediterranean and was a constant threat to Italy and the Venetian Empire. While he succeeded in evicting the Knights of St John from Rhodes he failed to oust them from Malta.

While his relationship with Francis I, King of France was cordial he had little regard for the Pope or Charles V, the Holy Roman Empire and his expansionist policies. When the Holy Roman Empire began to disintegrate at the time of the Protestant Reformation, Suleiman supported Protestant princes and countries against the Emperor and the Pope. Indeed, it is very likely that Protestantism would not have spread as far and as fast as it did without the support of the Ottomans.

Suleiman's legacy is not confined to military expansionism. During his reign he introduced many reforms and new canon laws. He broke with tradition by marrying a Christian concubine who then shared his private apartments instead of living in the harem, or *seraglio.* As his wife she became one of the most powerful women in Ottoman history taking a great interest in Suleiman's architectural and charitable projects.

Some of the greatest Ottoman architecture dates from Suleiman's reign. The Suleimaniye Mosque, for example, which still dominates the skyline of Istanbul, was commissioned by Suleiman and built by the famous architect Mimar Sinan. It is a blend of Islamic and Byzantine architecture that mirrors the Haghia Sophia, the imperial Byzantine church that was converted into a mosque by Mehmet II. (see chapter 4)

Suleiman commissioned work on the mosque complex in Mecca and the Dome of the Rock in Jerusalem. He also rebuilt and fortified the walls of Jerusalem, much of which can still be seen today.

He was a man both admired and feared; a man of few words and a tendency towards melancholia. He was a ruler of his age, alongside other great world monarchs and emperors of the time. Within a few years of his death in 1566, the Ottomans suffered a major defeat in 1571 at the naval Battle of Lepanto. This was to be the beginning of a slow decline in Ottoman power that continued until the Empire's dissolution in 1923.

CHAPTER SIX

Changing Balance of Power

Introduction

From the foundation of the Empire under Osman I in 1299, to the death of Suleiman the Magnificent in 1566, the Ottomans enjoyed a long period of growth and expansion. The next phase in their history was to be different.

Militarily, Ottoman expansion in Europe was to be checked by two major events; the Battle of Lepanto in 1571 and the Battle of Vienna in 1683. These two battles, one at sea and the other on land, resulted in resounding victories for the Christian nations and together marked a watershed in Ottoman military history.

During the same period the Empire's economy, particularly its centuries old trade with the East along the ancient Silk Route went into decline. This was partly due to the discovery by the Portuguese in 1488 of an alternative trade route to the Far East by sea around the Cape of Good Hope. The Portuguese then established trading posts in the Red Sea, Arabian Sea and Persian Gulf becoming a major challenge to Ottoman trade.

Battle of Lepanto 1571

Although the Knights of St John had successfully defended Malta from the besieging Ottomans in 1565, it had been a hard battle and was won at great cost. Having witnessed the strength of the Ottoman navy, the Knights and other European nations came to realise that if they were to eliminate the threat of the Turks this could only be achieved by a coalition force drawn from many nations. One country alone would never be capable of defeating the Ottomans.

In 1570 the Ottoman navy, under the command of Ali Pasha, laid siege to the island of Cyrus, which at that time was ruled by the Venetians. The Cypriot population of largely Greek Orthodox peasants, ruled by Venetian nobility, held out for over a year but the island was finally forced to surrender. Under the terms of capitulation, the Ottomans guaranteed that the Venetians would be free to leave the island and the local Cypriots would be unharmed. Despite this promise the Venetian commander, Marco Antonio Bragadin, was flayed alive and scores of Latin Christians were killed.

It is worth pointing out that during this period the Ottomans always showed a greater tolerance towards Greek Orthodox Christians than they did Western Catholic Christians, which included the Venetians. This attitude had been influenced by the Western Catholics' mistreatment of Orthodox Christians in 1204 when they sacked the city of Constantinople and established a Latin kingdom. Consequently, the Ottomans felt some affinity with the Greeks since both Greeks and Turks had a common enemy in the Western Catholic nations.

At the time, although the Ottomans were willing to trade with the Latin Christians such as the Genoese and Venetians, they always suspected the West and particularly the Holy Roman Empire, of expansionist and territorial ambitions.

After the siege and surrender of Cyprus by the Venetians in 1570 the island became part of the Ottoman Empire and remained so until 1878 when it came under British protection. However, the atrocities committed against the Venetians in 1570 and especially the brutal killing of Bragadin, so infuriated the Western European nations that they were determined to seek revenge. This led directly to the Battle of Lepanto.

On 7th October, 1571 an allied navy engaged the Ottoman navy in the Gulf of Patra in the Ionian Sea. The allies, organised by Pope Pius V and commanded by John of Austria, an illegitimate son of Charles V, comprised the Republics of Venice and Genoa, the Spanish Empire, the Papal States, the Grand Duchy of Tuscany, the Duchies of Savoy and Urbino and the Knights of St John.

Although the competing navies were fairly evenly matched in terms of ships and manpower, the battle was a resounding victory for the allies who lost less than 8,000 men and 17 ships compared with the Ottomans who suffered over 20,000 casualties and lost almost 200 ships.

The Battle of Lepanto is of significant historical importance in that it marked the last Mediterranean naval battle that was fought entirely by galleys and it was the first Ottoman defeat for over a hundred years.

Furthermore, both sides attached a religious significance to the event. The Ottomans could only come to terms with their defeat by claiming that it was the Divine Will of God, which must have been 'punishment' for their sins.

The Christians attributed their success in battle to the grace of the Virgin Mary who had answered prayers for victory. By way of thanksgiving the Pope instituted a feast day, known today as The Feast of Our Lady of Victory, which is still celebrated by Roman Catholics each year on 7th October, the anniversary of the Battle of Lepanto.

Battle of Vienna 1683

In 1529 Suleiman the Magnificent led his troops across the Balkans with the intention of taking Vienna. But after a two-week siege he retreated without engaging in battle. (see the previous chapter) However, because of its strategic importance on the Danube and its symbolic significance as the imperial city of the Holy Roman Empire, the Ottomans never gave up hope of conquering the city.

By the middle of the 17th Century the Habsburgs (the ruling dynasty of the Holy Roman Empire) were facing social, political and religious instability due to the rise of Protestantism. The movement started in Germany at the beginning of the 16th Century with the preaching of Martin Luther. It then quickly spread eastwards into Hungary and Transylvania posing a serious threat to the authority of the Catholic Church and the Empire.

In response the Papacy, supported by the Habsburgs, declared a Counter Reformation aimed at eradicating Protestant 'heresy', reinforcing Catholic doctrine and bringing Protestants back into the Catholic Church. Leopold I, the Emperor at the time, used particularly harsh measures in his determination to crush the Protestants in the Balkans. As a result, many looked to the

Ottomans for protection, an example being Imre Thokoly, King of Upper Hungary, who openly switched sides and swore allegiance to the Ottomans.

This naturally led to increased tension between the Habsburgs and the Ottomans. Kara Mustafa Pasha, Grand Vizier to the Sultan, believing the Habsburgs to be in a weakened position, advised that the time was ripe for another attempt to take Vienna. Despite the fact that Sultan Mehmet IV had reservations, preparations for another siege went ahead. Roads and bridges were repaired and munitions centres set up along the proposed route towards the Austrian capital.

On 21st January 1682 the Ottoman forces, reinforced by the Crimean Khanate, were mobilised under Grand Vizier Kara Mustafa. Heavy rain made the long journey from the Ottoman city of Edirne difficult and the carriages transporting the ladies of the harem often got stuck in the mud. Troops from Transylvania and Hungary joined the main army in Belgrade where the Sultan chose to break his journey. Unlike his predecessor Suleiman the Magnificent who led his troops on campaign and into battle, Mehmet IV chose to spend his time hunting in the woods of Belgrade.

Kara Mustafa's hope was that the Viennese would surrender in which case the Ottomans would inherit the entire wealth of the city. However, by August 1682 all negotiations had failed and therefore war was declared. But since the weather was bad and the campaigning season was almost over, battle didn't begin until many months later.

Such a long interval gave the Habsburgs time to both prepare their defences and seek allies who might come to their aid. Apart from reinforcing the city walls they demolished houses around the outskirts so creating an open space where attacking troops would be an easy target.

The Polish-Lithuanian Commonwealth immediately offered the Habsburgs support and overall command of the joint forces was given to the King of Poland, John III Sobieski. Other European states were too busy fighting among themselves and the French showed no desire to get involved in a Habsburg-Ottoman war.

Leopold, the Holy Roman Emperor, together with his court fled to Passau, a small town a little further along the River Danube. They took all the treasure they could carry with them. The Duke of Lorraine withdrew his troops towards Linz. This left just 15,000 men to defend the imperial city.

The siege began on 14th July, 1683 but it was to be two months before John Sobieski and his troops arrived by which time both the besieged and besiegers were on the point of exhaustion. The Viennese were running out of food, a situation not helped by the fact that hundreds from the surrounding towns and villages had sought refuge in the city so swelling the population. The Ottomans' supply lines were stretched to breaking point; their casualty rate was high and morale low.

On 11th September Sobieski's armies surprised Kara Mustafa by emerging unexpectedly from the forest with 20,000 Polish, German and Austrian cavalry. He led what is said to be the largest cavalry charge known in history and by the end of the following day it was all over. It is estimated that the Ottomans lost between 8,000 and 15,000 men in two days while the Christians lost some 3,500 lives.

The Christian forces chased the Ottomans back along the Danube towards Belgrade. The Ottoman camp was ransacked and everything of value, including livestock, was carried off. The greatest prize was the capture of Ottoman tents, some of which were made into liturgical vestments for the Church, others can still be seen in museums in Poland.

The Battle of Vienna was a humiliating defeat for the Ottomans. The Sultan blamed his Grand Vizier Kara Mustafa for the disaster. Consequently, the Grand Vizier was condemned and executed in the traditional manner: strangulation with a silk cord. In the meantime, the allied armies argued among themselves over the spoils of war.

The Polish-Ottoman War 1683-1699

Although the Ottomans were severely beaten at Vienna in 1683 the Christian nations still feared a counter-attack. In preparation for such an event Pope Innocent XI founded a Holy League incorporating the Holy Roman Empire, Poland and the Venetian Republic. Muscovite Russia joined in 1686, which was to be the first time that the Russians allied with Western forces.

Under Charles of Lorraine the Holy League drove the Ottomans back along the Danube, in the process capturing fortresses at Esztergom, Vac and Pest. In July 1686 the League, now including forces from England, Norway, Sweden and Italy managed to retake Buda, the western part of today's Budapest, after 143 years of Ottoman rule. Animosity towards the Ottomans by this time was so strong that once inside the city the imperial forces carried out a systematic massacre of both Muslims and Jews. It is estimated that some 3,000 Muslim men, women and children were killed and around 6,000 were taken as slaves. The Jewish population at the time numbered approximately 3,000. Half of these were killed and the other half taken into captivity. Both mosques and synagogues were destroyed.

In April 1687 the imperial forces, under Charles of Lorraine, marched towards Mohacs, another Hungarian city that had been captured by the Ottomans in 1526. At what is referred to as the Second Battle of Mohacs the Ottoman forces were soundly beaten once more, this time losing some 10,000 men compared with Holy League losses of just 600.

This second defeat within a period of one year and with such loss on the Ottoman side led to a crisis within the Empire. The commander of the troops, Suleiman Pasha deserted his men. The main army disintegrated. Even the previously loyal Janissaries disobeyed their senior officers and returned to Istanbul independently. When finally caught, Suleiman Pasha was executed. On 8th November, 1687 Sultan Mehmet IV was deposed and spent the rest of his life confined within Topkapi Palace.

Treaty of Karlowitz 1699

Over the next twelve years the Ottomans continued to lose territory to the Christian forces. Finally, in September 1697, a decisive battle was fought at Zenta, in today's Serbia that was to lead to the Treaty of Karlowitz.

On this occasion it was the Habsburgs, led by Prince Eugene of Savoy, who took the initiative by making a surprise attack on Ottoman forces as they crossed the River Tisa. It was to be the first of many victories for Prince Eugene. Once again it was disastrous for the Ottomans. They lost 30,000 men, 87 cannon, a train of camels, the royal treasury and the accompanying harem.

Just over a year later, in November 1698, the two sides met at Sremski Karlovci, modern Serbia, in order to negotiate peace terms. On 26th January, 1699, Rami Mehmet Pasha on behalf of the Ottomans and signatories representing the Holy Roman Empire, the Polish-Lithuanian Commonwealth, the Republic of Venice and Peter the Great, Tsar of Russia signed the Treaty of Karlowitz.

Under the terms of the Treaty it was agreed that each side should have rights to the territory they currently held. Consequently, the Habsburgs gained much of modern Hungary, Bosnia and Herzegovina, Croatia and Slavonia. Poland regained some of its lost territories and Venice acquired most of the Dalmatian coast.

The Principality of Transylvania remained nominally independent but it was subject to Austrian government, a pattern that was to be repeated in the Balkans for centuries to come. The situation in other Ottoman territories, and particularly rights to control the Holy Sepulchre in Jerusalem, was also discussed at the conference but no decisions taken.

The Ottomans kept Belgrade together with suzerainty over Wallachia and Moldavia.

Conclusion

The Ottoman siege of Cyprus in 1570 and brutal killing of Marco Antonio Bragadin along with other Venetians convinced the Christian nations that the Turks had to be defeated. In 1571 an allied navy under the command of John of Austria soundly defeated the Ottomans at the Battle of Lepanto, an event that is celebrated today as the Feast of Our Lady of Victory.

In 1683 the Ottomans suffered further humiliation at the Battle of Vienna. For the next 16 years the Holy League and the Ottomans fought for control of Central Europe until 1699 and the signing of the Treaty of Karlowitz. Under the terms of the Treaty the Habsburgs acquired large swathes of Central and Eastern Europe. The Habsburgs continued to rule the region either directly or indirectly under suzerainty for the next two hundred years. Discontent at Habsburg rule and calls for independence from Balkan nations were contributing factors towards the Balkan Wars of 1912 and the outbreak of the First World War in 1914.

It is interesting that the status of the Holy Sepulchre in Jerusalem, at that time in Ottoman hands, was also discussed at the Treaty of Karlowitz. Conflict between different Christian groups over access to the holy site contributed to the Crimean War in 1853 and will be discussed in a later chapter.

The Battles of Lepanto and Vienna clearly changed the balance of power in the region. For the first time since the founding of the Empire in the 13th Century the Ottomans were in retreat and losing large areas of European territory. The situation forced the Turks to embark upon a process of modernisation in order to be able to compete with the Habsburgs and other Western nations.

The psychological impact on the Ottomans of their changing role in the region was profound. Despite all efforts at reform and modernisation, from this point the Empire went into a steady decline until its final dissolution.

CHAPTER SEVEN

Fragmentation: Egypt, Greece and the Crimea

Introduction

The Ottoman economy suffered a severe blow to its Far Eastern trade via the overland Silk Road when the Portuguese discovered an alternative route by sea round the Cape of Good Hope in 1488. Then with the loss of large swathes of its European territory following the Battle of Vienna in 1683 their economy was weakened even further. Apart from losing the tax revenue that was traditionally imposed on the non-Muslim population, the Porte (Ottoman Government in Istanbul) also suffered a reduction in its supply of produce and manpower from territory lost to the Habsburgs.

All empires have problems governing their distant provinces and the Ottomans were no exception. They now found that with reduced resources and technology that lagged behind the West, the task became virtually impossible. The weakness of the Ottomans became evident in Egypt around the end of the 18th Century with the invasion of Napoleon Bonaparte and in the Crimea in the middle of the 19th Century.

As the Empire went into a steady decline the Western powers began to speculate about how Ottoman territory might be divided up should it finally collapse. The rise of Russia was a key factor in the equation.

Egypt and Napoleon

Egypt had come under Ottoman rule in 1517 when Sultan Selim I, known as 'the Grim', overthrew the *Mamluks* who at the time ruled Egypt, the Levant and the Hejaz. This brought the holy sites of Mecca and Medina into the Ottoman orbit. (see Chapter Five) The *Mamluks*, who were originally an army made up of slaves from Georgia, the Crimea and Circassia, became an elite military caste ruling Egypt from 1250 at which point they overthrew the *Ayyubids* and ousted the Western Crusaders. However, despite being conquered by the Ottomans in 1517, the *Mamluks* continued to be a powerful influence in Egypt and retained a certain amount of autonomy. From time to time they rebelled and attempted to take power back from the Porte. This naturally led to instability in Egypt.

Mamluk influence prevailed until 1798 when Napoleon Bonaparte invaded Egypt as part of his Middle Eastern campaign to conquer both Egypt and Syria. His motives were multiple. At the time Britain and France were competing for the Indian trade market. Napoleon believed that if he could secure a base in Egypt he would be in a better position to undermine Britain's access to India. He also claimed that French rule in Egypt would be beneficial to French scholars and scientists at a time when exploration of Egyptian antiquities was becoming popular. On a personal level, it has been suggested that he saw himself as a successor to Alexander the Great who had conquered Egypt in 332 BC and founded the city of Alexandria.

Napoleon landed in Alexandria on 1st July, 1798. He was reasonably successful with his land campaigns and even won a certain amount of popularity among the people by claiming to be their 'liberator' from the oppressive rule of the *Mamluks* and Ottomans. However, at sea the French suffered a major disaster when Rear-Admiral Horatio Nelson, commanding the British Fleet, defeated Napoleon's Navy at the famous Battle of the Nile that took place between the first and third of August.

After abortive attempts to take the coastal ports of Jaffa and Acre in today's Israel, Napoleon returned to Cairo with a depleted army, having lost almost 2,000 men either to the plague or having been killed in action. Many hundreds more returned wounded. Napoleon left Egypt in August 1799 leaving his troops behind. Finally, on 25th June, 1802, hostilities ended with the signing of the Treaty of Paris. Under the terms of the Treaty the Ottomans regained Egypt and the two powers retained good relations.

Egypt and Muhammad Ali

The signing of the Peace Treaty did not automatically bring peace however. Over the next three years a three-way civil war took place between the Ottoman Turks, the Egyptian *Mamluks* and Albanian mercenaries who were in the service of the Ottomans.

The Commander of the Albanians was Muhammad Ali Pasha. He took advantage of the power vacuum created by the civil war to shore up his own popularity and power base among leading Egyptian citizens, including the *ulema,* or religious establishment. By 1811 Muhammad Ali had eliminated the majority of the *Mamluks* and seized power for himself. Since the Ottomans were incapable at the time of ruling Egypt themselves they were forced to accept Muhammad Ali as *Wali* (Governor) of the country. The Albanian Commander eventually founded a dynasty that was to last until the Egyptian Revolution of 1952 when Gamal Abdel Nasser overthrew King Farouk.

Muhammad Ali immediately set about an ambitious reform programme aimed at modernising and Westernising the country. Whereas Ottoman attempts at reform failed due to obstruction by the conservative and powerful clergy, Muhammad Ali achieved considerable success in Egypt. He introduced measures to improve the economy, he reorganised the Government and above all be built a modern army with the help of the French.

Although Muhammad Ali ruled Egypt autonomously, technically he remained accountable to the Porte. On several occasions the Ottoman Government called upon him for support in military campaigns. This was the case, for example, in Saudi Arabia and the Greek Peninsula.

Saudi Arabia

While the Holy Cities of Mecca and Medina became part of the Ottoman Empire in the 16th Century, the interior of the peninsula remained largely in the hands of tribal leaders. In 1744 one of these tribal leaders, Prince Muhammad bin Saud formed an alliance with a radical preacher named Muhammad ibn Abd al-Wahhab so creating the Emirate of Diriyah, otherwise known as the First Saudi State.

In order to further seal the pact, a marriage was arranged between Abdul Aziz bin Muhammad, the son of bin Saud, and the daughter of al-Wahhab. The partnership between the monarchy of Saud and the religious authority of al-Wahhab remains the situation in Saudi Arabia to this day.

Both Muhammad bin Saud and al-Wahhab were determined to purge the entire Arabian Peninsula of what they saw as heretical practices such as pilgrimages to mosques and tombs and the worship of saints. Their extreme interpretation of Islam is known as Wahhabism or Salafism. (See my publication *Making Sense of Militant Islam*)

The Wahhabis were contemptuous of the Ottoman Sultan calling into question his legitimacy as *Caliph*. They frequently attacked Ottoman trade caravans and by 1805 had taken control of Mecca and Medina in the Hejaz.

In 1811 the Ottomans called on Muhammad Ali Pasha of Egypt to help oust the Wahhabis from the Hejaz and destroy their power in the peninsula. For the next seven years the Egyptian forces fought with the Wahhabis. Finally, in 1818, Ibrahim Pasha, Muhammad Pasha's son, secured the surrender of Abdullah bin Saud who was sent to Istanbul and executed. This was to be the end of the First Saudi State. In 1824 Turki bin Abdullah bin Muhammad, a grandson of the first ruler, expelled the Egyptian forces from Riyadh and founded the Second Saudi State.

Greece

Ever since the fall of Constantinople and the collapse of the Byzantine Empire in 1453, Greeks had remained the largest non-Muslim group in the Ottoman Empire. The majority of these Greeks lived on the Greek Mainland, the Greek islands and the Peloponnese. However, a large number had always lived in Constantinople where they held important government posts such as that of dragomen (interpreter). They also held key positions in the Ottoman navy.

Over the centuries there had been sporadic Greek rebellions against Ottoman rule. In March 1821, with encouragement from Russia, a serious rebellion broke out in the Danubian Principalities of Moldavia and Transylvania that quickly spread to the Peloponnese, Central Greece, Crete and Macedonia, which were all Ottoman territories at the time.

The Porte's response to such a vast insurrection was to call once again on the help of Muhammad Ali Pasha of Egypt. The Egyptians agreed to come to the Porte's aid but only on condition that they be given territory. Ibrahim Pasha, son of Muhammad Ali Pasha, sailed for Greek waters in July 1824. By the end of 1825 most of the Peloponnese, as well as Athens, was back in Ottoman hands. The city of Missolonghi fell in April 1826 following a yearlong siege.

Both sides committed large-scale atrocities. But reports of Ottoman barbarity, some of it exaggerated, were soon circulating in the Western Press. Dramatic paintings such as Eugene Delacroix's *Massacre of Chios* depicting the suffering of the Greeks at the hands of the infidel caused an outcry among the general public. Volunteers from European countries, including the poet Lord Byron who met his death in Missolonghi, fought alongside the Greeks. Following increasing calls for intervention on behalf of the Greeks, the Great Powers of France, Britain and Russia finally decided to send in their navies.

On 20th October, 1827, after a weeklong stand-off, the allies engaged the Ottoman navy that was supported by vessels from the provinces of Egypt, Tunis and Algiers. The location of the battle was Navarino Bay (modern Pylos). Remembered as the famous Battle of Navarino it was to be the last major sea battle fought entirely between sailing ships. The result was the total destruction of the Ottoman fleet and a resounding victory for the allies. With the help of the French the Ottomans were finally pushed out of the Peloponnese. Greece was recognised as an independent nation under the Treaty of Constantinople in May 1832 and the allies installed Bavarian Prince Otto von Wittelsbach as the first monarch of an independent Greek Kingdom.

Following the defeat of the Ottomans at the Battle of Navarino relations between the Sultan and Muhammad Ali Pasha of Egypt deteriorated, partly because Ali Pasha believed that he had been cheated out of promised territory. His next move was to send his son Ibrahim to conquer Ottoman Syria. After taking Acre, Damascus and Homs, Ibrahim entered Anatolia reaching as far as Konya.

Ibrahim remained as Governor of Syria until 1838 when the Ottomans began to fight back retaking their territory. At this point Britain and the Austrian Empire intervened on the side of the Empire and Ibrahim was forced out of Syria and back to Egypt in February 1841.

The Rise of Russia

By the middle of the 19th Century it was quite clear that foreign powers were interfering in Ottoman affairs. This began in a serious way following the Battle of Vienna in 1683 when Austria started to push the Ottomans back along the Danube seizing territory as they went. However, it was the rise of Russia that changed the balance of power in the region causing both Britain and France, and to a lesser extent Austria, the greatest concern.

It was under Peter the Great (1672-1725) that Russia's territorial ambitions became evident. In his determination to drag the Tsardom of Russia from its backward feudalism into the modern Western world, Peter toured Europe in order to learn all he could about Western modernisation. He travelled to the Netherlands to study shipbuilding and he went to England where he met King William III and visited Greenwich. He also went to Manchester, considered to be a model city, the architecture of which would later influence his own city of St Petersburg.

The greatest problem for Russia at the time was limited access to the sea. The only outlet was the White Sea on the North East coast, which was closed to shipping during the winter months due to thick ice. His other options were the Baltic, at that time in the hands of the Swedish Empire and Black Sea, which would give him access to the Mediterranean through the Dardanelles. The problem was that the Ottomans controlled the Black Sea.

In order to secure a port on the Black Sea Peter would have to expel the Tartars of the Crimea whose Khan was a vassal of the Sultan. His first attempt, in the summer of 1695, to take the Ottoman fortress of Azov ended in failure. He then began a programme to improve and enlarge his navy using the skills learned in the Netherlands. The following year, in 1696 he returned with a fleet of some thirty ships. This time he was successful and the Sea of Azov passed into Russian hands.

Under Catherine the Great, who ruled from 1762 to 1796, the Russian Empire continued to expand. Catherine was equally, if not more, determined than Peter to extend her Empire. But Catherine's ambitions went beyond territorial acquisition. Catherine was strongly religious and envisioned the revival of the Byzantine Empire. She wanted all Orthodox Christians across the Balkans to be united under the Russian Church. She also hoped to restore the mosque in Constantinople to its former glory as the Haghia Sophia, mother Church of Orthodoxy.

Treaty of Kucuk Kaynarca 1774

Various wars were fought during the 18th Century between the Russians and Ottomans for control of the Black Sea. The 1768-74 Russo-Turkish War ended with the Peace Treaty of Kucuk Kaynarca, known today as Kaynardzha in modern Bulgaria. The Treaty was to have major implications for the Ottoman Empire.

Under its terms the Danubian principalities of Wallachia and Moldavia were returned to the Ottoman Empire. Despite this the Russians maintained the right to intervene in the principalities in cases of misrule by the Ottomans. The Treaty also allowed for Russian merchant vessels to have free access to the Dardanelles. The Crimean Khanate, though nominally independent, in reality became dependent upon Russia and in 1783 was formally annexed to Russia under Catherine the Great.

Crucially however, it was to be the religious issue that was to have the greatest influence over later developments. Eastern Orthodox Christians were given the right to sail under the Russian flag. But above all, the Russians gained the right to protect all Orthodox Christians living in the Ottoman Empire, a right that they were to use to their advantage on numerous occasions in the future.

The Crimean War

Selim I conquered the Holy Land as part of his Middle Eastern campaign in 1517 and from that time onwards the Ottomans held the holy sites of Jerusalem and Bethlehem as well as the Muslim

Holy Cities of Mecca and Medina. When Russia acquired a favoured status following the Treaty of Kucuk Kaynarca in 1774, this gave her advantages in the Holy Land over and above other Christians, especially the Roman Catholics.

Relations between the Western Catholics and Eastern Orthodox had never been good, culminating in the schism in 1054 when the Church split into two branches; the Western Church under the Pope in Rome and the Eastern Church under the Patriarch in Constantinople. After the Sack of Constantinople by Western Crusaders in 1204, when hundreds of Orthodox Christians were massacred, the situation deteriorated even further.

The status of Jerusalem was particularly sensitive. When the Crusaders conquered the city in 1099 a Crusader Kingdom was established and a Norman French King put on the throne. For a hundred years the French ruled the Kingdom of Jerusalem until ousted by *Salah ad-Din Yusuf,* known in the West as Saladin. The crusaders then moved to Acre where they stayed until 1299, when the *Mamluks* finally expelled them from the Holy Land.

Despite having ruled Jerusalem for only a hundred years and then being ousted by the *Mamluks,* the French Catholics never lost their sense of ownership of the Holy City. Therefore when the Russians were given special privileges by the Ottomans under the terms of the Treaty of 1774, the French were affronted. The French appealed to the Porte to reverse the terms of the Treaty of Kucuk Kaynarca. They said that they could never accept the Russians as protectors of their interests in the Holy Land, a land that they themselves had ruled for two hundred years. This put the Ottomans in a difficult position. They were caught between the Russians and the French, each country with its own agenda and each prepared to use the Ottomans to further their own ambitions.

For centuries Russian pilgrims had made the journey overland or by sea across the Eastern Mediterranean to the Holy Land. By the end of the 18th Century Russians represented the largest Christian pilgrim group far outnumbering all others, including the French.

Western pilgrims visiting the city found the ways of the Eastern Christians strange. Apart from language, food and dress, they criticized the Russians for being backward, over emotional, loud and disrespectful in the churches. But more seriously, rumours began to circulate that the Russians were becoming too powerful in the region. There was even talk that they were planning to overthrow the Ottomans.

There was some justification in fearing Russia's territorial ambitions regarding the Ottoman Empire. Both Peter and Catherine the Great had never hidden their expansionist intentions. Catherine had spoken openly with the Austrians of her hopes of carving up the Ottoman Empire and her great dream was to restore the holy cross to its true place on top of the great Church of Hagia Sophia in Constantinople.

Fueled by the French and English Press, anti-Russian feelings grew. Although Russia always claimed that her only interest was to protect the rights of Greek Christians in the Balkans or other parts of the Ottoman Empire, the great powers suspected that Russia's true motives were pure expansionism. Both France and Britain had trade interests in the Empire and neither country wanted to see it fall to the Russians. Britain also feared that a strong Russia would threaten her Indian trade. The Austrians feared that Russian presence in the Balkans could lead to inter-communal tensions resulting in violent reprisals by Muslims against Christians.

France and Britain decided that the only way to combat the Russian threat would be to support the Ottomans, who by this time were being referred to as the 'sick man of Europe', a term that has been ascribed to Tsar Nicholas I. It was against this background that France and Britain decided to support the Ottomans against the Russians. Consequently, when Russia invaded Ottoman territory in the Danubian principalities in June 1853, France and Britain immediately sent their war ships to the region.

The stifling heat of the Danube Delta, plus an outbreak of cholera, enabled the Ottomans and her allies to push back the Russians. Perceiving a potential power vacuum in the principalities Austria sent her forces in, ostensibly to maintain peace and protect the Christian population. In reality Austrian presence in the Balkans was to remain until the outbreak of the First World War.

With Russia ousted from the Danube delta there was a chance to negotiate peace terms. The allies offered the Russians peace conditional upon accepting four points: a) that Russia renounce any special rights in Serbia and the Danubian principalities, b) that navigation of the Danube should be free to all commerce, c) that there should be an end to Russian domination of the Black Sea, d) that Russia should abandon its claim as protectorate over Christians in Ottoman territories.

Even if Russia had been prepared to accept these terms, which she was not, there were strong voices in the British Parliament and among the public that Russia should not be allowed to get away so easily. There were calls for military action to destroy Russia's naval power in the Black Sea once and for all. When the Russians finally left the principalities in late July 1854, the allied forces were already heading for Sevastopol, home of the Russian Fleet.

What became known as the Crimean War lasted until March 1856, during which time major battles were fought in the Danubian principalities: Sevastopol in the Crimea, the Caucasus and the Baltic. Out of a total number of over 900,000 allied forces, including the Ottomans, almost 300,000 were killed in action. The Russian forces numbered just over 700,000. Some 140,000 were killed in action with thousands more wounded.

Russia finally sued for peace in March 1856 and the war officially came to an end with the signing of the Treaty of Paris on 30th March, 1856.

Conclusion

The 19th Century proved to be a time of great upheaval across large parts of Europe, the Balkans and the Arab countries, in the process of which the Ottomans lost a great deal of territory. Napoleon's failed attempt to take Egypt, which was at the time an Ottoman Province, left a power vacuum that the Ottomans were unable to fill. Instead the country came under the rule of Albanian Commander, Muhammad Ali Pasha, who was to found a dynasty that lasted until the 20th Century.

Perhaps the most significant event, however, was the rise of Russia. Both Peter and Catherine the Great had never hidden their ambitions of conquering Ottoman territory and restoring the Byzantine Empire. When Russia was granted special rights by the Ottomans to act as Protector of Greek Christians in Ottoman lands she used the privilege to further her own ends.

Russia was supportive of the Greek rebellion against the Turks. The Greek freedom fighters formed a secret society, known as *Filiki Eteria* (Friendly Society) that was based in Odessa. The leader of the movement, Alexander Ypsilantis, was a General serving in the Russian Army, which is just one example of the close links between Russia and Greece.

The Russians invaded the Danubian principalities in 1853 on the grounds that they were protecting Christian subjects of the Ottoman Empire. However, Britain and France believed the invasion to be the beginning of their long-term strategy to conquer Ottomans lands. The allies therefore agreed to support the Ottomans in their fight against the Russians.

When the Russians were expelled from the principalities, Austria moved in claiming to be peacemakers and protectors of the

Christians. France and Britain suspected that Austria's true intention was to regain and hold on to territory that had been in Ottoman hands for centuries. Their suspicions were not groundless.

By 1854 it had become clear that the Allies' intentions were less about defending the Ottomans and much more about stopping the territorial expansion of Russia and reducing her naval power.

Throughout this period France, Britain, Austria and Russia at various times planned among themselves how the Ottoman Empire should be divided up once 'the sick man of Europe' had finally collapsed. Sixty years later, following a far greater war, a world war, the Ottoman Empire was indeed divided up.

CHAPTER EIGHT

End of Empire

Introduction

The Crimean War was to be another turning point in the history of the Ottomans, as had been the case with the Battle of Vienna in 1683, the Treaty of Kucuk Kaynarca 1774 and the Battle of Navarino in 1827. In all cases these events resulted in a changed relationship with the Western powers that was generally to the detriment of the Ottomans.

Such events convinced the Sultan of the need to modernise the army along Western lines and in 1826 the Janissaries were disbanded in favour of a modern military force. In 1839, in an effort to stem the rise of nationalism in the provinces and particularly the Balkans, the Porte introduced a series of reforms, known as the *Tanzimat*, meaning 'reorganisation'. An important part of these reforms included a change in the status of non-Muslims whereby all citizens of the Empire, regardless of religion or ethnicity, would be equal under the law. It was hoped that these changes would address both the calls for reform demanded by the outside powers and at the same time better integrate the minorities as full Ottoman citizens.

Other interesting reforms included the abolition of slavery and the slave trade and also the decriminalisation of homosexuality, a reform that was far ahead of many Western countries. The *Tanzimat* also included the founding of several colleges of further education, the first post office and the first bank notes.

The financial burden of these reforms, plus the cost of the Crimean and other wars, put the Ottomans into debt and forced the Porte to accept foreign aid. In 1875 the Empire was officially declared bankrupt.

Along with financial and economic problems, political instability continued in the Balkans. Austria-Hungary annexed Bosnia Herzegovina in 1908, an event that led to the assassination, in 1914, of Archduke Franz Ferdinand of Austria and his wife Sophie, Duchess of Hohenberg while they were on a visit to Sarajevo. The murder of the heir to the Austria-Hungary throne triggered a series of events that culminated in the outbreak of the First World War, which finally resulted in the dissolution of the Empire.

Reform

Sultan Murad I formed the Janissary Corps in 1383. (see Chapter Two) The Corps, which included the Sultan's personal army, initially recruited from Christian prisoners of war and slaves from Greece and Albania. Following a period of strict training and indoctrination the recruits joined an elite and well-disciplined fighting force. By the end of the 16th Century Turkish Muslims were also being enrolled into the Corps, bringing the total number of Janissaries to around 49,000. The numbers then rose sharply at the beginning of the 19th Century to approximately 135,000.

From the 16th Century onwards corruption became commonplace and discipline was difficult to enforce. Eventually the Janissaries become a power in their own right and their influence on the Porte, the Sultan and the palace grew. When Sultan Selim III attempted to bring in a series of reforms in 1807 the Janissaries rebelled and deposed him.

In 1826 Sultan Mahmud II once more attempted reform, announcing that he was going to form a new army that was to be trained and organised along Western lines. As predicted, the Janissaries rebelled and marched on the Sultan's palace. In response loyal troops set fire to the Corps' barracks resulting in the death of 4,000 Janissaries. Many others were killed in street fighting across the city. Those who survived either fled or were imprisoned. The leaders were executed and the Janissary Corps was officially disbanded.

The reform of the military was just one part of an on-going process of reform that began in 1839 and ended in 1876 with the First Constitutional Era. While the military reforms were clearly aimed at bringing the Ottoman forces up to the same standard as those of the Western powers and particularly Russia, the majority of the other reforms related to the minorities living within the Empire.

As mentioned in the previous chapter, foreign powers and especially Russia, had justified intervention in Ottoman affairs on the grounds of protecting the Christian minorities. One consequence of this was that Christians across the Balkans were encouraged to rebel against their Ottoman overloads. Another was a rise in nationalism across the Balkan provinces.

The Porte believed that if it could improve the lives of the minorities, the Western powers would have less justification for intervention. At the same time, it was hoped that the reforms would lead to the minorities being better integrated into Ottoman society.

One of the earliest Decrees was the Treaty of Gulhane in 1839. This abolished the *millet* system whereby minorities had operated autonomously within their own religious community. By ending the *millets* all citizens regardless of religion would have equal status under the law. The *dhimmi* system, whereby all non-Muslims had to pay a special tax to the government, was also abolished.

While this was presented as an advantage, some minorities rejected the idea on the grounds that they would lose their special privileges such as being exempt from military service.

Countdown to War

The annexation of Bosnia-Herzegovina by Austria in 1908 led to a rise in nationalism in the Balkans. It was in this context that the Serbian nationalist Princip Gavrilo assassinated the Austrian heir to the throne, Archduke Franz Ferdinand, on 28th June, 1914. The Austrians responded on 28th July by declaring war on Serbia. A few days later, on 31st July, Russia mobilised her troops in readiness to protect Serbia against Austria, an act that prompted Germany to declare war on Russia on 1st August. On 2nd August, Germany invaded Belgium and on the following day declared war on France. At this point Britain declared war against Germany. Bulgaria was persuaded to join the Central Powers (Austria-Hungary and the German Empire) the following year, in September 2015.

For several decades Germany had been providing the Ottomans with military expertise and training as part of the Sultan's reform programme. Germany also financed the Anatolian railway connecting Istanbul, Ankara and Konya and the proposed Berlin-Baghdad Railway. The plan was that the line should run through the Ottoman territory of present day Turkey, Syria and Iraq with the aim of establishing a port in the Persian Gulf. Due to the outbreak of the First World War the line was not fully complete until 1940.

It was not surprising therefore that although the Empire initially professed neutrality the Ottomans were eventually drawn into the war on the same side as Germany.

The Sykes-Picot Agreement, May 1916

By November 1915, just over a year from the time war was first declared, France, the United Kingdom and Russia, known as the Triple Entente, were predicting that the fall of the Ottoman Empire was inevitable. Secret discussions began in the November regarding the future of Ottoman territory and continued until March 1916. Mark Sykes, on behalf of the United Kingdom, and Francois Georges-Picot on behalf of France conducted the talks with the agreement of Russia. The conclusions were set out in a final agreement that was signed on 16th May, 1916.

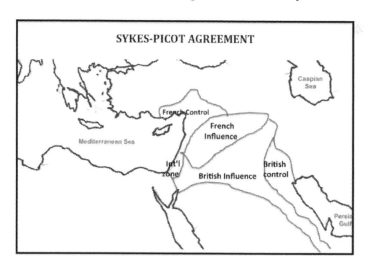

There had been considerable debate, some of which was heated, regarding how territory covering today's Syria, Iraq, Jordan and Lebanon should be divided up between France and the United Kingdom. Discussions also included the future of Jerusalem and the Arab tribes of the Hejaz.

The Agreement immediately created a conflict of interest in three particular areas: first, it was contrary to the policy of non-intervention in the affairs of the Maronites, the Orthodox Christians, Druze and Muslim communities of the Levant. Second, it was contrary to the promises of Arab independence made by Britain through the efforts of diplomat/military officer/archaeologist T E Lawrence, popularly known as 'Lawrence of Arabia' whose story is depicted in the film of the same name. Third, the Agreement went against the spirit of self-determination that was championed by American President Woodrow Wilson.

The Sykes-Picot Agreement was initially kept secret. However, after the Russian Revolution in 1917 and the subsequent fall of Tsarist Russia the Bolshevik government rejected Russia's claims under the Agreement and released a copy of the text to the public. Copies were soon circulating in the British and French press causing outrage in some quarters.

The Zionists were annoyed by the Agreement since its publication came just three weeks after the Balfour Declaration which was a letter written by British Foreign Secretary James Balfour to Walter Rothschild, a prominent leader of the British Jewish community. In the letter, dated 2nd November 1917, the Foreign Secretary stated:

His Majesty's government view with favour the establishment in Palestine of a national home for the Jewish people, and will use their best endeavours to facilitate the achievement of this object, it being clearly understood that nothing shall be done which may prejudice the civil and religious rights of existing non-Jewish communities in Palestine, or the rights and political status enjoyed by Jews in any other country.

Both the Sykes-Picot Agreement and the Balfour Declaration were to have major repercussions for the future of the Middle East. Indeed, it could be argued that the current instability in the region can be traced back to these two documents.

The Armenian Massacre

In the decades leading up to the outbreak of war, relations between Christians and Muslims deteriorated. This was partly fuelled by the fear, to some extent justified, that Christians were collaborating with their co-religionists in Russia. Indeed, there were some Armenians who saw an opportunity for achieving their own independent state should Russia win the war.

Russia circulated anti-Ottoman propaganda among the Armenian population and went as far as arming insurgents. As a result, the government suspected Armenians of treachery and decided to take drastic action. On 25th February, 1915 the Porte ordered that all Armenian soldiers enlisted in the army should be disarmed. On 24th April, 1915 it was decided to deport all Armenians living near the Ottoman-Russian front line to Syria and Iraq in order to prevent collaboration with the Russians.

In the middle of May 1915 a Russian-Armenian 'army' attacked the Ottoman garrison at Van and massacred the population before establishing an Armenian 'State'. On the 27th May the Government reacted by passing the 'Deportation Law' whereby all Armenians were forcibly marched from the region of Van and other areas with significant Armenian populations, to South East Anatolia and Syria.

Although strict instructions had been given regarding their safe passage, hundreds either died of hunger or exhaustion or were murdered on the journey. Those who did survive went through terrible suffering. It is estimated that between 800,000 and 1.5 million Armenians died in what is referred to as the Armenian Genocide. Many hundreds more, including professionals and intellectuals, were imprisoned. To this day the Republic of Turkey has refused to acknowledge that the Armenian deaths were an act of genocide or that the Ottoman administration was culpable. It is an issue that has caused on-going friction between the Turkish Government and the West.

Armistice of Mudros, October 1918

The Russian Revolution in 1917 and the fall of the Tsarist Empire had a significant effect on the course of the war in the region. For a short time, the Ottomans benefited from the Revolution because it was possible to regain some previously lost territory during the subsequent power vacuum. However, the capitulation of Bulgaria with the signing of the Armistice of Salonica on 19th September, 1918, dealt a severe blow to the Central Powers. Under the terms of the armistice the Bulgarian army was disarmed and demobilised and German and Austrian troops were forced out of Bulgaria. This paved the way for French troops to move into Romania while British and Greek troops advanced towards European Turkey. It was only a matter of time before the Allies would be at the walls of the ancient city of Constantinople.

The defence of Constantinople without the help of the Bulgarians was virtually impossible. After talks in Berlin and Sofia with the Germans and Bulgarians, the Grand Vizier Talaat Pasha returned to Constantinople to advise his government that defeat was inevitable. It was decided that the Porte should discuss peace terms with the Allies and that the current government should be disbanded in the hope that terms of surrender would be less harsh than they might have been with the government that took the Empire into war.

The armistice was signed on 30th October in Mudros harbour on the Greek island of Lemnos. The negotiations were conducted by Admiral Calthorpe for the British without the presence of the French. The following day hostilities between the Ottoman Empire and the Allies came to an end.

Under the terms of the Armistice the Ottoman army and navy were demobilised. Garrisons other than those in Anatolia surrendered and the Allies had the right to occupy forts in the Dardanelles and Bosphorus. The most significant clause however gave the Allies the right to occupy any Ottoman territory 'in case of disorder' that might pose a threat to their security. The Greeks were later to use this clause as justification for invading the hinterland of Anatolia in 1919.

Immediately following the armistice French, British and Italian troops took over Constantinople. This was the first time the city had been occupied by a foreign power since the Ottoman conquest of 1453.

The Sultanate was abolished on 1st November, 1922 and the Caliphate on 3rd March, 1924 when the last *Caliph*, Abdulmecid II, went into exile.

The Treaty of Sevres

On 10th August, 1920 delegates from the Allied Powers and the Ottoman Empire met at Sevres, a suburb of Paris, in order to sign what became known as the Treaty of Sevres.

The Treaty marked the official partitioning of the Ottoman Empire. To a large extent the new borders of today's Syria and Iraq reflected the same proposals as were set out in the Sykes-Picot Agreement of 1916. France received the mandate for Syria and Lebanon and Britain was given the mandate for Iraq and Palestine. Under the terms of the San Remo Conference in April 1920 Britain also assumed control of Transjordan, a situation that remained in force until 1946.

Significant territory was assigned to Greece, including most of Thrace as far as the ancient Ottoman capital of Edirne, parts of Anatolia around the city of Izmir and the islands offshore. Italy received the Dodecanese Islands and parts of South Western Anatolia; the cities of Antalya and Konya, also came under Italian influence.

The Kingdom of Hejaz was granted international recognition, which went some way towards fulfilling British promises for Arab independence in return for Arab support in fighting the Ottomans during the Arab Revolt. However, in 1925 the Kingdom was conquered by the Sultanate of Nejd and in 1932 was incorporated into the Kingdom of Saudi Arabia.

Of special interest is that under the terms of the Treaty of Sevres provision was made for an independent Armenia, which would have complied with the spirit of self-determination advocated by United States President Woodrow Wilson.

Consideration was also given at the time to the provision of an independent territory for the Kurds. However, since ethnic Kurds straddled different geographic areas and political entities, no agreement could be reached as to where the boundaries of an independent Kurdistan should be.

Under the terms of the Treaty navigation through the Dardanelles, the Bosphorus and the Sea of Marmara became free to all shipping at all times, so becoming international waters. Despite the harsh measures imposed upon the Ottomans, their delegates had little option but to sign the Treaty.

The Treaty of Sevres was never fully ratified. Greece refused ratification because she disagreed with the suggested borders. Furthermore, the terms were unacceptable to the growing number of Turkish nationalists who had been active for several years before the outbreak of war, a situation that was to lead directly to the Turkish War of Independence.

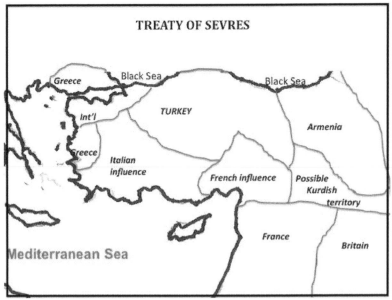

Conclusion

Faced with the loss of large parts of the Empire, a failing economy and increasing foreign intervention, Sultan Selim III and his successor Mahmud II introduced a series of drastic reforms. Reform of the military and laws relating to the religious minorities were the most significant.

The Janissary Corps, which by the early 19th Century was both corrupt and overly powerful, was opposed to any kind of reform. Following a major rebellion in 1826, the Sultan decided to disband what had once been an elite fighting force that was both feared and respected by the West.

Reforms relating to the religious minorities, included the abolition of the *dhimmi* status and the *millets,* resulting in all citizens, regardless of religion, being conscripted into the army. This policy backfired at the beginning of the war when Armenian soldiers, on the grounds of being potential traitors, were disarmed, demobilised and either imprisoned or executed.

The Ottomans sought the aid of the Germans to help modernise and train its new army. German expertise was also used to build the infrastructure such as roads and railways. It was not surprising therefore that with the outbreak of the First World War the Empire found itself on the same side as Germany despite initially claiming neutrality.

As early as the reign of Catherine the Great at the end of the 18th Century, both Russia and Austria spoke openly about conquering Ottoman territory. Throughout the 19th Century, as the Empire gradually lost both land and influence, speculation increased among the Western powers as to what should happen to the Empire, particularly beyond Anatolia, once the 'Sick Man of Europe' had finally breathed his last breath.

Soon after the beginning of the First World War Britain and France were in secret negotiations over the partition of the Levant culminating in what became known as the Sykes-Picot Agreement. However, the proposals contained in the Agreement conflicted however with the Balfour Declaration, a document signifying Britain's support for an independent Jewish state.

The Ottomans capitulated in October, 1918 and the Allies met to discuss peace terms at Sevres on the outskirts of Paris. The Treaty of Sevres was finally signed on the 10th August, 1920. It established the boundaries of today's Syria and Iraq, mirroring the proposals laid down in the Sykes-Picot Agreement. Britain and France competed for control in the region in order to protect their trade interests.

The interests of Greece and Italy were also reflected in the Treaty. Greece had never given up hope of regaining Constantinople and restoring the Christian 'Byzantine' Empire. Under the terms of the Treaty she received both Thrace and large parts of Anatolia around Izmir. Italy received islands and coastal regions of Anatolia, areas that she once held during the period of the Venetian Empire.

The terms of the Treaty were harsh on the Empire, which was now seen by the West as a backward degenerate and dysfunctional entity. What is interesting is that only sixty years earlier both Britain and France had fought alongside the Ottomans against Russia in the Crimean War. However, that was less about protecting a 'friendly' ally than halting the growing power of Russia.

Two other points of interest were the proposal for an independent Armenia and Kurdistan, neither of which materialised. Following the Armenian Massacres, also known as the Armenian Genocide or Armenian Holocaust, many Armenians went into diaspora. In 1922 the territory of 'Armenia' was absorbed into the Soviet Union. The question of the Kurds, who still straddle Turkey, Syria, Iraq and Iran, remains with us today, as does the Kurdish dream of a homeland.

Perhaps the most significant consequence of the Sykes-Picot Agreement and subsequent Treaty of Sevres was the decision to create countries with boundaries that were drawn across lines in the sand regardless of ethnic, linguistic and tribal considerations. The situation was then compounded by the imposition of pro-

Western rulers who had not been chosen by the people. Ultimately this contributed to the 2011 Arab Spring and the ideology of *Daesh*, the so-called Islamic State, whose aim is to reverse the Sykes-Picot Agreement and restore the *Caliphate*.

The immediate effect of the collapse of the Ottoman Empire, particularly in the Levant, will be discussed in the following chapter.

CHAPTER NINE

The Aftermath

Introduction

Following the armistices that ended the First World War in 1918, world leaders and diplomats from around 30 countries met at the Paris Peace Conference in January 1919 in order to discuss peace terms. American President Woodrow Wilson also attended the Conference where he put forward his policy of the right of nations to self-determination. Negotiations were to continue for twelve months, until January 1920, during which time various Treaties were finalised.

One of the most significant outcomes of the Paris Peace Conference was the founding of the League of Nations on 20th January, 1920. The primary aim of the League was to maintain peace through the collective action of its members and to act as arbitrator in cases of dispute.

Under the auspices of the League of Nations, Class 'A' mandates were granted to Britain and France. Britain received mandates for Mesopotamia (Iraq) and Palestine with Transjordan while France was given the mandates for Syria and Lebanon.

The Treaty of Sevres that was signed by representatives of the Allied powers and the Ottoman Empire on 20th August, 1920 marked the beginning of the official partition of the Empire. Under the terms of the Treaty the Ottomans lost all their territory apart from Central Anatolia thereby even losing access to the Mediterranean Sea.

These harsh terms were unacceptable to the nationalist movement that was led at the time by Mustafa Kemal, later known as Ataturk. Under his leadership the Turks went to war in May, 1919 against the Allies in what is known as the Turkish War of Independence. Ataturk's forces managed to liberate those parts of Anatolia that had been awarded under the Treaty to Greece and Italy. After three years of fighting the Republic of Turkey was declared on 29th October, 1923 and Mustafa Kemal became its first President.

During the years leading up to, and during the First World War, thousands of Muslims fled the Balkans to seek refuge in Anatolia while Christians left Ottoman lands for the safety of Greece. However, in January 1923 a formal exchange of population, based on religion, was agreed between Greece and Turkey resulting in the forcible exchange of approximately two million people.

The Mandates

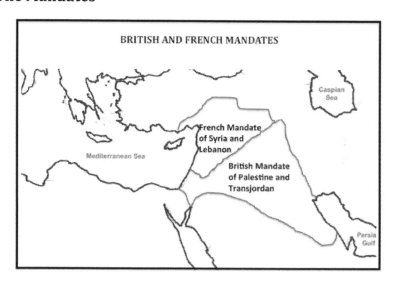

The Mandates were awarded by the League of Nations in cases where sovereignty had been removed from a territory and the people were not "able to stand by themselves". They were awarded to Allies who "by reason of their resources, their experience or their geographical position" were best able to fulfill the task of a mandatory power. Mandates differed from Protectorates in that with the former, territory was temporarily placed under the tutelage of another power until such time that the people were considered able to rule themselves. A Protectorate on the other hand retains a certain amount of local autonomy but remains under the sovereignty of a greater power for an indefinite period.

Class 'A' Mandates related specifically to former Ottoman territory while Class 'B' Mandates covered former German territory and her colonies. In all cases the mandatory powers were accountable to the League of Nations and were not permitted to build military fortifications or raise armies.

Although the aim of the Mandates was to enable territories to move towards independence, the presence and oversight of Western powers was highly unpopular among the people and usually led to uprisings.

Paris Peace Conference

Negotiations between Britain and France at the Paris Peace Conference concerning the future of Syria and Iraq were frequently heated. Both countries had their own agendas. France had a history in the Levant going back to the Crusades and still saw herself as protector of the Christian minorities, particularly in Lebanon with whom she had good relations. The Mandates for Syria gave France an opportunity to acquire Damascus, a city that had escaped her during the Crusades and the French would also gain access to the Eastern Mediterranean through the Mandate for Lebanon.

Lloyd George, the British Prime Minister at the time, was overheard at the Paris Peace Conference muttering to himself: "Mesopotamia...yes...oil...irrigation...we must have Mesopotamia; Palestine...yes...the Holy Land...Zionism...we must have Palestine; Syria...h'm...what is there in Syria?" (*Peacemakers*, Margaret Macmillan, p.392)

When Lloyd George and Georges Clemenceau, Prime Minister of France, met in London on one occasion, it is reported that they had a short, light-hearted exchange as follows:

"Well" said Clemenceau, 'what are we to discuss?'

Lloyd George replied, 'Mesopotamia and Palestine'.

Clemenceau: 'Tell me what you want?'

Lloyd George 'I want Mosul.'

Clemenceau: 'You shall have it. Anything else?'

Lloyd George: 'Yes I want Jerusalem too.'

Clemenceau: 'You shall have it but Pichon [French Foreign Minister], will make difficulties about Mosul. (*Peacemakers*, Margaret Macmillan, p.392)

Once the potential oil wealth of Mosul became apparent Britain, France and also the new Republic of Turkey competed for its reserves. Turkey claimed rights to drilling in Mosul on the basis of previous agreements. The Kurds of the region also put forward a claim. The case was finally taken for arbitration to the League of Nations who judged in favour of Mosul coming under the British Mandate of Iraq, so reflecting the 1916 Sykes-Picot Agreement. However, the share of oil and the route of proposed pipelines linking Mosul with the Mediterranean continued to cause tension between the British and French for some years.

Mandates of Iraq and Syria

One of the first acts of the British in Iraq was to dismiss Ottoman officials and form a new administration staffed largely with British officers. Consequently, many Iraqis saw themselves becoming part of the British Empire. This was a fear shared across Iraqi society and united both the Sunni and Shi'a in peaceful demonstrations and calls for independence.

In June 1920 the Shi'a cleric Ayatollah al-Shirazi issued a *fatwa* justifying the use of arms on the grounds of defending Iraqi rights to self-determination in accordance with the policies laid down by Woodrow Wilson. Armed revolt broke out and quickly spread across the region of the lower Euphrates. In response the British sent in reinforcements, including two squadrons from the Royal Air Force that were based in Iran. The rebellion was finally quashed in October 1920 at a cost of around 8,000 Iraqi and 500 British lives.

The rebellion caused the British to review their policies in Iraq. It was decided to invite Emir Faisal bin Hussein of the Hashemite dynasty to rule as King. Faisal was a son of the Grand Sharif of Mecca and had collaborated with the British and T. E. Lawrence during the Arab Revolt against the Ottomans in 1918. He was with the Allies when they marched into Greater Syria and took control from the Ottomans. Faisal became King of Syria on 9th March, 1920 on the grounds that Britain had promised Arab independence in exchange for Arab support against the Ottomans.

Unfortunately, the following month Syria was then awarded as a Mandate to France under the terms of the Treaty of Sevres. When French troops moved into Syria to take up their Mandate they met resistance from the Arabs. This led to the Franco-Syrian War that lasted between March and July 1920. The French finally defeated the Syrians at the Battle of Maysalun on 24th July. The monarchy was abolished and King Faisal was sent into exile. His period as King of Syria had lasted just four months and sixteen days.

Understandably the British decision to install Faisal as King of Iraq in August 1921, just a year after the French sent him into exile, was not well received and relations between the two countries deteriorated. When France faced rebellions against its rule in Syria she suspected British involvement and accused Britain of harbouring Syrian rebels over the border in Iraq and supplying them with finance and arms.

Lebanon

The French Mandate for Syria and Lebanon was divided into various territories. Apart from Syria it included the State of Greater Lebanon, the Alawite State and Jabal Druze State. The State of Greater Lebanon was established on 1st September, 1920 with the aim of providing a 'secure' region around Mount Lebanon for Christian Maronites who had enjoyed a certain amount of autonomy under the Ottomans. At the same time the French reduced Syria by enlarging Lebanon to include the Bekka Valley, the Mediterranean ports of Tyre, Sidon, Tripoli and land just North of Palestine. Beirut became the capital.

The result was that thousands of Muslims now found themselves being dominated by a minority Christian elite who were closely allied to the French. The loss of Syrian lands to Lebanon and growing religious tensions were to contribute to the various political and military conflicts that plagued Lebanon over the following decades.

On 1st September, 1926 Lebanon became a republic and achieved full independence from France when the French Mandate ended on 24th October, 1945. Syria achieved independence on the same date.

At that time there were several secular socialist parties vying for power in Syria, one being the Arab Ba'ath Party. A 16 year-old Alawite student named Hafez al-Assad joined the Party in 1946, a year after independence. In March 1971 Hafez became President of Syria and was succeeded on his death in 2000 by his third son Bashar al-Assad who remains in office to this day.

Iraq achieved independence on 3rd October, 1932 and Faisal remained as king from the time of his enthronement in August 1921 until his death in 1933. The succession remained within the Hashemite dynasty until the monarchy was abolished in 1958 when Iraq became a republic. In 1968 the Ba'ath Party overthrew the Presidency and in 1979 Saddam Hussein became the fifth President of Iraq.

Transjordan

Of all the Mandates, that of Palestine and Transjordan was probably the most complex. When Britain received the mandate for Palestine in 1923 it covered two distinct areas: the region west of the River Jordan, known as Palestine and east of the River Jordan referred to as Transjordan. Palestine remained under British Administration until 1948 when the State of Israel declared itself independent. Transjordan was semi-autonomous until 1946 when it became an independent nation known as Jordan.

The British installed Emir Abdullah I as ruler of Transjordan. He was the second son of Hussein bin Ali, Sharif of Mecca of the Hashemite dynasty. Like his brother Faisal, who became King of Iraq, Abdullah worked with the British against the Ottomans during the Arab Revolt. He was with General Allenby and T. E. Lawrence when they entered Jerusalem in 1917 and when the country became independent in 1946 he became the first King of Jordan.

Abdullah was assassinated at the Al Aqsa Mosque in Jerusalem in 1951 in the presence of his grandson Hussein. Abdullah's son Talal succeeded to the throne but was King for just one year. He abdicated due to ill health in favour of his son Hussein. Hussein ruled for over forty years until his death in 1999 when his son Abdullah II succeeded as King and remains on the throne to this day.

Palestine

By installing Faisal, first as King of Syria and then Iraq, and his brother Abdullah as Emir and then King of Jordan, the British hoped that they were going some way towards fulfilling their promise of self-determination for the Arabs. It was a vain hope in the light of the Balfour Declaration that supported a homeland for the Jews. In other words, Britain was trying to reconcile two competing interests: a homeland for the Jews and independence for the Arabs, to be created on the same relatively small strip of land.

When Britain's intentions became apparent both sides felt cheated resulting in the rise of nationalist insurgences. The British found themselves in an invidious position. They were trying to keep the peace not only between angry and disaffected Muslim and Jewish groups who fought each other, but also from those on both sides who were against British rule and its policies.

In 1936 the Arabs rose up in revolt against both Jewish immigration and British rule. A Commission of Inquiry was set up to investigate the situation and reported back in July 1937. The findings of the report, known as the Peel Commission, stated that the Mandate was failing and therefore recommended partition of the country. Three different plans were suggested but the Arabs rejected them all. Hostilities resumed and continued until 1939 by which time some 5,000 Arabs, 400 Jews and 200 British had been killed.

In an attempt to appease the Arabs and maintain peace, Britain introduced new legislation restricting Jewish immigration. Unfortunately, the timing of the decision coincided with the outbreak of the Second World War. Despite this, British ships off the coast of Palestine turned away thousands of illegal Jewish refugees who were fleeing the horrors of the holocaust.

From 1940 onwards Britain faced increasing attacks from Zionist groups. The most serious was in 1946 when Urgun, a Zionist paramilitary organisation, blew up King David Hotel in Jerusalem killing 92 people. Since it was the headquarters of the British administration many British were killed. In 1948 another Zionist group assassinated a UN mediator. By this time Mandatory Palestine had become increasingly unpopular in both the United States and Britain where the public was highly critical of the cost, both in lives and money, of keeping 100,000 British troops in the territory.

In 1947 civil war broke out between Jewish and Muslim communities and British forces seemed unable to restore peace. From this point British police gradually withdrew, handing over responsibility for peacekeeping to the Jewish forces. Early in 1948 Britain announced her intention to end the Mandate no later than 14th May. That same day Israel declared independence. Jordan then annexed the West Bank and East Jerusalem. Egypt seized the Gaza Strip and 700,000 Palestinians fled the country.

Conclusion

At the Paris Peace Conference delegates had the task of implementing the various peace treaties and reconciling the competing claims for territory that were being put forward. Although American President Woodrow Wilson had stressed that his policy of self-determination should be adhered to, other considerations took priority. For example, access to oil and the route of a proposed pipeline from Mosul to Haifa determined the borders between the new states of Iraq and Syria, an issue contested between Britain and France. And Britain was keen to acquire the Mandate for Palestine that would enable her to protect British interests in the Suez Canal. What seems clearly evident is that decisions on boundaries were based on the interests of the Allies. The will of the people was largely disregarded.

Perhaps the only slight exception to this was in the case of a Jewish homeland. Once the Balfour Declaration became public Britain could no longer ignore the growing voices, both in the United States and from the Jewish community at home, for an independent nation for the Jews. But the creation of a Jewish homeland could only come at the expense of reneging on the Arabs.

Certainly the Mandate for Palestine proved to be the most difficult to administer. Britain faced an impossible task by trying to satisfy both parties. In an attempt to appease the Arabs, she installed Kings Faisal and Abdullah in Iraq and Transjordan respectively. The hope was that since both came from the ancient Hashemite dynasty, which descended from the line of the Prophet Muhammad, they would be acceptable to the people. This worked in the case of Transjordan but not Iraq.

It is almost a hundred years since the fall of the Ottoman Empire. All that is left in Turkish hands of its former vast territory is the area of today's Republic of Turkey. Nearly every other region has faced instability and war, from the Balkan Wars of 1991 to 2001, the various Lebanese and Arab-Israeli Wars, and currently the upheaval following the Arab Spring that started in 2010, the effects of which continue today. In the light of decisions made by the West following the First World War it is interesting to speculate how many of these conflicts can be directly attributable to Western decisions and Western intervention

EPILOGUE

Today the hot spot of unrest is Syria, the repercussions of which are reverberating across the Western world. From the outbreak of the Syrian Civil War in early 2011, it has been estimated that as at February, 2016, the total number of deaths due to the war stood at some 470,000.(Syrian Observatory for Human Rights) Internally displaced persons are given as over 7,600,000 with over 4,000,000 people made refugees.(United Nations Commissioner for Refugees)

The current blame for this disaster is being placed upon three main parties: the brutal regime of the Syrian President Bashar al-Assad, the various rebel groups who rose up against his rule, and *Daesh*, the terror group that is also known as the so-called Islamic State. All three share some culpability, a situation that has hindered efforts at resolving the conflict.

The root causes of the problem are very deep and can be traced back to the dissolution of the Ottoman Empire and subsequent Peace Treaties that were ratified by the Allies, as well as Western interference over recent decades.

The creation of the Mandates resulted in large swathes of Arab territory coming under mandatory French or British rule, a direct result of which led to a growth in Arab nationalism. Furthermore, many Arabs in the region were angered by what they perceived to be Britain's duplicity. Instead of achieving Arab independence, as had been promised, in return for helping to defeat the Ottomans, their lands were carved up and they were placed under foreign rule with a 'puppet sovereign' from another tribe being placed on the 'throne'.

While elements of Arab nationalism can be traced back to calls for independence during the Ottoman period, the ideology gained force at the time of the Mandates and spread across the Arab world. The Declaration of the State of Israel in 1948, resulting in the displacement of an estimated 711,000 Palestinians (United Nations Relief and Works Agency for Palestine), further strengthened the resolve of the Arab peoples to preserve and protect Arab identity and fight for sovereignty.

Arab nationalism suffered a severe blow in June, 1967 during the Six Day War between Israel and an allied army of Egyptian, Syrian, Jordanian, Iraqi and Lebanese forces. Against all odds Israel not only defeated the Arabs but at the same time she annexed the Sinai Peninsula including the Gaza Strip from Egypt, the West Bank from Jordan and the Golan Heights from Syria. These annexations led to the further displacement of Palestinians, with hundreds of thousands fleeing from the West Bank into Jordan, from the Gaza Strip into Egypt and from the Golan Heights into Syria.

This mass exodus added to the general instability in the region. The influx of refugees into neighbouring countries following the Six Day War only added to the refugee problem that had been created by the displacement of refugees in 1948 and the Arab/Israeli war of 1958. After 1967 refugee camps, particularly in Lebanon, became even more overcrowded. They have always been natural breeding grounds for discontent and the nurture of insurgency groups. These camps still exist and the refugee problem facing Lebanon in particular is more critical than ever as the tiny country struggles with the arrival of a further 1,500,000 refugees as a result of the current Syrian Civil War.

Today's mass exodus of refugees from Syria, Iraq and other war torn countries of ex Ottoman territory has led to a crisis across Europe and fed into the debate on immigration that influenced the United Kingdom's recent decision to leave the European Union.

Apart from the continuing refugee problem, the dispute over territory between Israel and the Palestinians has still not been resolved. Both sides claim territorial rights. While Israel may appeal to Biblical tradition, both Israel and the Palestinians base their claims on the various Documents and Treaties of the post Ottoman period, the most significant being the Balfour Declaration and the Sykes-Picot Agreement.

Crucially, however, those Palestinians who have remained in Israel, the West Bank or the Gaza Strip see themselves as living under an illegal occupation. This is a view that is shared across the Muslim world in general and the Arab world in particular. The plight of the Palestinians is like a running sore. Until it is healed it continues to infect relations between many Muslim countries and the West, which by and large is perceived to support Israel.

Gamal Abdel Nasser, President of Egypt (1956-1970), had hoped to unite the Arabs of the region as peoples sharing a common language and culture. This was known as Pan-Arabism. However, after the Six Day War and defeat of the allied Arab forces, his hopes were dashed. Equally, nationalism espoused by individual Arab states, was not succeeding. With the failure of pan Arabism and nationalism, which were both secular movements, people now turned to the religion of Islam, or Islamism, as a way forward.

Strands of Islamism can be detected throughout Islamic history. However, the current phenomenon can be traced to the doctrines of *Wahhabism* and *Salafism* that took root in Saudi Arabia in the 18th Century. In the early 20th Century nationalists living under British and French Mandates, as well as those opposed to the British presence in Egypt, for example the Muslim Brotherhood, gradually turned to Islamism. With the suppression and imprisonment of members of the Muslim Brotherhood in Egypt in the middle of the 20th Century, and other activists opposed to the State of Israel, some of the leading thinkers and advocates of Islamism sought refuge in Saudi Arabia.

One such was *Abdullah Yusuf Azzam* who left Palestine to take up a teaching post at King Abdul Aziz University in Jeddah where he taught that militant *Jihad* was an obligatory duty of all Muslims. *Azzam* was teaching at the university during the late 1970s when *Osama bin Laden,* one of the founders of *Al Qaeda,* happened to be a student at the same university. It is quite likely that this is when *Bin Laden* first came under the influence of *Azzam* and his militant views.

It is possible to draw a straight line from *Osama bin Laden* to *Daesh.* When the Soviet Union invaded Afghanistan in December 1979 *Bin Laden* volunteered, along with hundreds of other young Saudis, to support their Muslim brothers in the fight against the Russians. By 1988 he had gathered a band of followers together who became known as *Al Qaeda* ('the Base'). During this same period the West provided him with arms to fight the Russians.

When the Soviets left Afghanistan in 1989 *Bin Laden* returned to Saudi Arabia where he was greeted as a hero. He toured the country giving speeches about the injustices suffered by Muslims around the world: Palestinians under the Israelis, the Chechens under the Soviets and the Bosnians at the hands of the Serbs. In 1990 *Bin Laden* offered to lead his 'Afghan army' against Saddam Hussein following the invasion of Kuwait. However, he was rebuffed by the Saudi Monarchy in favour of the protection of the United States. The sense of rejection and humiliation, coupled with his anger at the prospect of American boots on the ground in the 'Land of the Two Holy Mosques', would have a profound effect on *Bin Laden*.

Following the New York attack on the Twin Towers on 11th September, 2001, *Bin Laden* was the key suspect. Ten years later, in May 2011, United States Intelligence Forces tracked him down in Pakistan and shot him dead. Although *Bin Laden* had been executed, the *Al Qaeda* ideology remained alive and well. Indeed, it became even more of a threat as *Al Qaeda* members dispersed to all parts of the world.

The search for *Bin Laden* started in Afghanistan but the war against terror very quickly moved to Iraq. When the United States invaded Iraq in 2003 on the grounds that Saddam Hussein was harboring weapons of mass destruction, many *Al Qaeda* operatives travelled there to fight the invading and occupying Western forces. They were known as *Al Qaeda* in Iraq (AQI). In 2006 AQI merged with other Sunni militant groups to form the Islamic State of Iraq (ISI).

Soon after the outbreak of the Syrian Civil War in 2011, *Abu Bakr Al-Baghdadi,* the leader of the Islamic State of Iraq, began sending *Al Qaeda* fighters across the border into Syria where they formed the *Al Nusra* Front with an affiliation to *Al Qaeda.* In April 2013 *Al Nusra* merged with the Islamic State of Iraq becoming known as 'The Islamic State of Iraq and *al-Sham* (ISIS). The following year, in June 2014, *Al-Qaeda* broke with ISIS, which now called itself the

'Islamic State' (IS). *Al Baghdadi* became *Caliph*. Since the majority of Muslims do not recognise the legitimacy of the 'Islamic State' the organisation is more commonly referred to by the derogatory term *Daesh*. (For a more detailed account see my book *Making Sense of Militant Islam*.)

A few points are worth mentioning here. First, before the West's invasion of Iraq in 2003, there was no obvious *Al Qaeda* presence in the country. As mentioned above, *Bin Laden's* protégés went to Iraq after the US invasion in order to fight the Americans. The United States and her allies not only toppled Saddam Hussein but also disbanded Iraq's military forces and destroyed the country's infrastructure. Consequently, *Al Qaeda* and its successor *Daesh* filled the vacuum. Furthermore, displaced Iraqi army officers joined the ranks of *Daesh* and weapons captured from the Western forces were added to its arsenal.

Second, the fact that *Daesh* is far more extreme than *Al Qaeda* and has been criticised by mainstream Muslims as being un-Islamic, has not deterred many hundreds of young men and women from around the world travelling to Syria to join the terror group. These recruits are being indoctrinated into the hard line ideology that was propounded by *Abdullah Yusuf Azzam,* friend and mentor to *Bin Laden.* Perhaps more importantly, their commitment to militant *Jihad* is fed on the plight of the Palestinians and injustices of the post Ottoman Peace Treaties that robbed the Arab Muslims of their land. Indeed, one of the stated aims of *Daesh* is to restore the Ottoman *Caliphate* under a new *Caliph*.

Third, it is relatively easy for members of *Daesh* to cross the border from Iraq into Syria and neighbouring countries. Cells now exist across the Levant and Southern Turkey, with a large presence in Libya. This ease of movement is not surprising when we consider that for centuries the region was all part of the Ottoman Empire. Countries such as Iraq, Syria and Libya are less than a hundred years old. The borders that were put in place in the post Ottoman period are meaningless to many of the tribal peoples of the region. The British and French discovered this during the Mandate period when both sides accused the other of harboring terrorists.

Turning now to the Balkans, although the region was not put under foreign rule after the dissolution of the Empire, it nevertheless has suffered periods of instability, much of which can be traced back to the middle of the 19th Century. Most of the conflicts in the Balkans are rooted in ethnic and religious differences, for example the Yugoslav Wars between 1991 and 2001.

Throughout most of the history of the Empire these differences were subsumed under the Ottoman policy of pluralism. However, ethnic and religious differences began to emerge from the 17th Century onwards as the Ottomans lost territory to the Habsburgs. When Austria, Russia and to a lesser extent Britain, encouraged and supported the Christians of Ottoman Europe to rebel against their Muslim Masters, religious identity became critical.

During the final decades of the Empire violent conflict between Christians and Muslims broke out, very often with Jews caught in the middle. Unspeakable atrocities were committed by all sides as the Ottomans fought for survival. For some Greek, Armenian, Jewish and Turkish people, the suffering experienced is still within living memory. It has fed into a fear and prejudice of the other that remains to this day, albeit perhaps just beneath the surface. It is perhaps not surprising therefore that some of the Balkan countries, for example Macedonia, Serbia and Hungary, have taken a hard line against the plight of largely Muslim refugees fleeing the current Syrian crisis. In many cases rather than finding safety they have discovered their paths blocked by walls of barbed wire.

The final few words must be given to the Republic of Turkey, a state that was created out of the rump of the dying Empire. Kemal Ataturk, who became the first President, was convinced that the Ottomans had fallen behind the West largely because they were held back by their conservative religion of Islam. He was determined therefore that the new Republic would be based on secular values. In this he has been largely successful but in recent years Turkey has witnessed a resurgence of Islamic observance, evidenced by an increase in the wearing of the hijab and the building of mosques. It has even been suggested that the current President aspires to reinstate the *Caliphate* with himself as *Caliph*.

The course of history follows the principle of cause and effect. Turkey has come a long way since 1923 but she is still haunted by the ghost of the Armenian tragedy and the problem of how to deal with the Kurds, both issues that were exacerbated by the fall of the Ottoman Empire. The refugee crisis that we are witnessing today can be traced back to the post-Ottoman period. It is a crisis that threatens the stability of Europe and the survival of the European Union.

*****

GLOSSARY

Abbasid: Islamic dynasty from 750 to 1258 with capital in Baghdad

atabeg: Hereditary title of Turkic nobility

bey: Turkic chief or noble

beylik: Territory ruled by a *bey*

Caliph: Successor to the Prophet

dervish: Member of Muslim religious order following vows of poverty

devsirme: Collection of young Christian boys as form of taxation

dhimmi: Religious minorities given protection under Ottomans on payment of tax

divan: Government body

Emir: Governor of Province

fatwa: Legal opinion/pronouncement

ghazi: Muslim warrior

Grand Vizier: Prime Minister to Sultan

Hajj: Annual pilgrimage to Mecca

ilkhanate: Area ruled by a Khan (king)

jizyah: Special tax paid by religious minorities

khan: Ruler or king

qadi: Islamic judge

madrassa: Islamic school or college

Mamluks: Sultanate ruling from Cairo (1250-1517) originating from slaves

millet: Religious minority organised into a community

rashidun: 'Rightly Guided Ones' during the period of the First Four Caliphs

Salafi: Those who advocate a return to the first three generations of Muslims

spahi: Turkish irregular cavalry

Sultan: Ruler, title of authority

Umayyad: Islamic dynasty ruling from 661 to 750 with capital in Damascus

ulema: Religious scholars

Wahabbi: Conservative religious movement originating in Saudi Arabia

Wali: Governor of administrative region

WORKS REFERRED TO

Halil Inalcuk, *Turkey and Europe in History*, 2006, Eren

Misha Glenny, *The Balkans,* 1999, Granta Books

Margaret MacMillan, *Peacemakers,* 2001, John Murray

Davied W. Lesch and Mark L. Haas, Editors, *The Middle East and the United States* 2012, Westfield Press

Caroline Finkel, *Osman's Dream,* 2005, John Murray

James Barr, *A Line in the Sand,* Simon & Schuster

Jason Goodwin, *Lords of the Horizons,* Vintage Books

Orlando Figes, *Crimea; the Last Crusade,* Allen Lane

Printed in Poland
by Amazon Fulfillment
Poland Sp. z o.o., Wrocław

49279222R00058